W9-CQH-467

How to be a graphic designer, without losing your soul
New edition
Adrian Shaughnessy

Princeton Architectural Press, New York

Published in 2010 by
Princeton Architectural Press
202 Warren Street
Hudson, New York 12534

Visit our website at www.papress.com

Published simultaneously by Laurence King Publishing Ltd, London

21 20 19    8 7 6

For Princeton Architectural Press:
Project editor: Nicola Bednarek

Special thanks to: Nettie Aljian, Bree Anne Apperley, Sara Bader, Janet Behning,
Becca Casbon, Carina Cha, Tom Cho, Penny (Yuen Pik) Chu, Carolyn Deuschle,
Russell Fernandez, Pete Fitzpatrick, Jan Haux, Linda Lee, Laurie Manfra,
John Myers, Katharine Myers, Steve Royal, Dan Simon, Andrew Stepanian,
Jennifer Thompson, Paul Wagner, Joseph Weston, and Deb Wood of
Princeton Architectural Press—Kevin C. Lippert, publisher

Library of Congress Cataloging-in-Publication Data
Shaughnessy, Adrian.
How to be a graphic designer, without losing your soul / Adrian Shaughnessy. —
New ed.
    176 p. : ill. ; 23 cm.
Includes bibliographical references and index.
ISBN 978-1-56898-983-9 (alk. paper)
1 . Graphic arts—Vocational guidance. 2. Commercial art—Vocational guidance.
I. Title.
NC1001 .S53 2010
741 .6023—dc22
                                                    2010010954

Typeset in Berthold Akzidenz Grotesk
Printed in China

*Seeing comes before words.*
John Berger,
*Ways of Seeing*

4

Contents

## How to be a graphic designer, without losing your soul

No one was more surprised than me when the first edition of this book started to sell in healthy quantities around the world. We're not talking *Da Vinci Code* numbers here, but since *How to be a graphic designer, without losing your soul* first appeared in 2005 it has been translated into seven different languages and has brought me into contact with some remarkable people, mostly individuals and groups I wouldn't otherwise have met.

I wrote the book in 2004, and much has happened since then. To hardened watchers of the international graphic design scene it sometimes feels like being on a high-speed train and seeing stations snap past so quickly that there isn't time to read the names of the stations. No sooner had the first version of this book appeared than parts of it felt out of date. I wrote it before web design became the primary occupation of many thousands of graphic designers; I wrote it before the digital realm threatened every aspect of media hegemony; I wrote it before blogging software created writers out of countless designers; I wrote it before the widespread renewal of interest in design with a social focus; and I wrote it at a time of relative abundance—plenty of work for everyone and plenty of opportunities for employment among graduates and young designers.

But it's not only graphic design that has changed since the relative calm of 2004: the entire world has changed. In 2008 there was a global financial crisis that caused every developed nation to look into the abyss. I can remember waking up every morning and switching on the radio only to be sucked into the snake pit of impending financial collapse. People we'd been urged to admire and envy—the bankers—suddenly appeared to be no better than bandits in a wild west movie; politicians who had extolled the virtues of unregulated financial markets suddenly looked like seedy racecourse bookmakers who had just seen the rank outsider win a dozen races; the financial innovations that we'd been encouraged to think of as dazzling examples of human genius, turned out to be not much better than fraud.

After months of this, however, my gloom eventually lifted and was replaced by a new optimism. Yes, we taxpayers were going to be paying for the banker's hubris for decades to come; yes, some designer friends had lost their jobs; and yes, I suffered a scary drop in my own income as an independent designer and writer. But beyond the worry and despondency, I saw something else. I saw a growing revulsion for the pursuit of money and a rekindling of interest in the common good. I saw an interest in looking afresh at the way we live and the way we earn our daily bread.

Surprisingly, I saw this most clearly in the many design schools I visited. Previously there had been an all-consuming interest among students and graduates in joining the style wars and producing stylistically radical work, but I now found a new interest in doing work that had a pronounced social focus. Suddenly, an obsession with design's purely stylistic qualities felt selfish and backward looking, and instead, young designers (and some older ones) were asking themselves—How can I use my design skills to make the world a better place? Suddenly, it was hip to be looking at ways of using design to prevent crime, to stop waste, and to benefit all members of society and not just the cool design-loving elites.

I recently encountered an interesting example of design skills being used to drive social change. I heard about three students from fashionable London design schools who'd taken on the task of reclaiming a strip of public land near a housing project. According to one of the trio, Richard Knowles, the exercise was a way of bringing the community together. "At the start we weren't sure what we wanted to do. We approached them with a few ideas for how to redevelop a communal space that was not being used and this started a dialogue between the residents and us. We saw this as a good way of bringing the community together to think about how they could use this green area."

So far, so good, but surely someone who had studied urban planning or one of the social sciences would be better placed to help? I wanted to know how a graphic design education had benefited the group in their task. "I think it helped us to visualize our ideas so we could continue that dialogue with the residents," said May Safwat, another group member. 'We made countless diagrams and models and took them to community meetings and it helped the residents understand where we were coming from". Knowles was equally clear that graphic design skills were an essential part of the process: "Whether this is a graphic design project or not, it comes down to a process. Start with research, finding problems and thinking about ways to solve those problems. We continually talked with the residents; they know the area better than us and really we came up with a solution that they had thought of but didn't quite know how to express themselves visually".

A few years ago these students might have hoped to use their skills to design CD covers or identities for art galleries or theaters, yet here they were working on a project with a purely social focus. It felt like a big change in what it means to be a graphic designer, and takes us back to a time—the early years of the twentieth century—when the Modernists saw design as a democratizing and inspiring force for good.

And yet, much as I welcome this new development in design, I am someone who is fixated with shape and color, form, and texture. In other words, the look of things. For me, the message isn't always what matters: graphic design doesn't always have to be "solving problems" or embodying well-tooled business strategies, or even performing a useful practical purpose such as signage or information delivery. If graphic design can do these things and still be visually captivating—which it often can—then so much the better, but sometimes it's enough that it is a thrilling arrangement of letterforms, shapes, colors, and imagery. One of my favorite books is an old battered paperback from the 1970s of mainly German logos. I barely recognize any of the companies or institutions represented and therefore remain unaware of the strategy behind, or appropriateness of, the hundreds of marques on display. Yet I get a thrill looking at these well-formed, incisive pieces of graphic expression. I like the look of them.

To have a visual sensibility means that the appearance of things is sufficient reason to appreciate visual design. But of course, this view is anathema to many designers—and clients —who only recognize design that has a purpose and a conceptual underpinning. This is all well and good, but the sad fact is that more often than not, this leads to dull design and the visual expression of sameness and uniformity. We only get truly great work when designers retain an intuitive and visionary approach. And as I've argued repeatedly with clients, the best way to get a message across is to be different.

## How to be a graphic designer, without losing your soul

I'd add one more reason why a preoccupation with the "look of things" is justified. My sense of history is based largely on a reading of the visual codes of past times, and nowhere is this stronger than in the modern era—the era of graphic design. Few elements of life evoke periods, flavors, and memories more potently than graphic design. When I look at some austere geometric letterforms by Wim Crouwel or a psychedelic poster by Martin Sharp, I get a vivid recreation of the times that the work comes from, and it's every bit as evocative as written texts, the fashions of the period, or photographic records.

Jonathan Barnbrook alludes to this way of reading the culture in his interview on page 126. He talks about the influence of psychogeography on his work, which he defines as the effect on the emotions and states of mind of our geographical environment. He says: "Graphic design is one of the major ways this is transmitted to me. It can be an old sign somewhere or the small details you see when you go to a new city; we all react emotionally to these things, in a way often quite unintended by the designer. I try to put these feelings in particular into my typefaces. It's quite hard to explain—feelings of nostalgia, ennui, some quite painful, some to do with a beauty that has been lost, but they are all because of the ephemeral and prominent nature of design. There is an attempt in my work to express it to other people. This is the one where I hope to connect in a different, less quantifiable, logical way".

This is my view, too: graphic design is part of the psychological, cultural, and physical ecosystem we live in, and this book is an attempt to assist people who see the world in a similar way. But as the reader you are entitled to ask: in what way is this book different from the first edition? Well, it has been extensively rewritten. Outdated and irrelevant material has been pruned and new avenues have been explored. In addition there are two new chapters (2 and 8) dealing with the major changes that have taken place within design. One thing is unchanged, however: it is still a book for those designers who, as I wrote in my original introduction (see p. 12), "believe that graphic design has a cultural and aesthetic value beyond the mere trumpeting of commercial messages."

In the years since I wrote those words, being that sort of designer has become more, not less, difficult. To produce work that has worth and meaning has become a struggle. And yet, with the cultural changes that have been brought about in many parts of the world by the banking crisis, I think that the struggle might become less arduous in the coming years. There is plenty of evidence to show that people are fed up with ungovernable wealth creation, wars fought on false premises, the destruction of the planet, and ruthless me-me-me behavior. Maybe, just maybe, there is an opportunity to be a designer with preoccupations other than being a force for consumerism or commercial propaganda.

I hope that anyone who shares this view of graphic design will consider that this is a fight worth fighting. This book is offered as a map of the battle terrain and provides survival tips and a few ideas to help avoid becoming a casualty of the graphic design wars.

**How to be a graphic designer, without losing your soul**

I love being a designer. I love thinking about ideas freely and observing them taking shape; I love working concentratedly on a project all day, losing myself in the work, and, even after having been involved in this field for almost twenty years, I still love getting a piece back from the printer (if it turned out well).

There are so many fantastic designers working today: creators like Jonathan Barnbrook and Nicholas Blechman who emphasize the social role of design; designers who produce breathtaking forms, such as M/M in Paris, Nagi Noda in Tokyo, and Mark Farrow in London; designers who blur the boundaries between design and technology like John Maeda, Joachim Sauter, and their students; and a new generation who manage to work with one foot in the art world and the other in the design world, like the young Swiss group Benzin and the American designers involved in the "Beautiful Losers" exhibition, including Ryan McGinness and Shepard Fairey.

I recently taught the spring/summer semester at the University of the Arts in Berlin, and was happy (and a bit astonished) to see how smart the students were. They are better educated, more widely travelled and more culturally astute than my generation was. On the same note, the range of students I currently teach in the graduate design pro-gramme at New York's School of Visual Arts includes a biology major from Harvard and a senior designer from Comedy Central.

There is also a new emphasis on how design is reviewed and critiqued, driven by Steven Heller's Looking Closer series, *Emigre* magazine's reconfigured essay-heavy format, Rick Poynor's *No More Rules* and *Obey the Giant*, and maybe most significantly, by the emergence of design blogs like underconsideration.com and designobserver.com. I don't think there ever was a time when design was reviewed so critically and enthusiasti-cally by so many people in so many cultures.

Of course, as it became a wider discipline, graphic design became more diffi-cult. It now embraces what used to be a dozen different professions: my students com-pose music, shoot and edit film, animate, and sculpt. They build hardware, write software, print silkscreen and offset, take photographs, and illustrate. It's easy to forget that routine jobs like typesetting and color separation used to be separate careers. A number of schools have realized this and opened up the traditional boundaries between graphics, product design, new media, architecture, and film/video departments, encouraging the education of a truly multifaceted designer.

For me, it has become more difficult, too: as I get older I have to resist repeating what I've done before; resist resting on old laurels. Before the studio opened in 1993, I was working at M&Co., my then favorite design company in New York. When Tibor Kalman decided to close up shop in order to work on *Colors* magazine in Rome, it didn't feel right to go and work for my second favorite design company. So I opened my own studio, and concentrated on my other great interest, music. I had experience working for both tiny and gigantic design companies and having enjoyed the former much more than the latter, I tried hard not to let the studio grow in size.

I feel a lot of designers starting out want to be concerned only with design and find questions about business and money bothersome. The proper setup of a studio and the presentation of a project to a client—in short, the ability to make a project happen—is, of course, as much a part of the design process (and much more critical to the quality of the process and the end product) as choosing ink colors or typefaces.

I learned a lot from my time at M&Co. They had used timesheets, for example, and I thought, if it's not too square for them, it can't be wrong for me. I am glad I did too; it's the only way to find out if we made or lost money on a project. If I'm not on top of the financial details, they will soon be on top of me and I won't have a design studio any more. It is much cheaper to sit on the beach and read a book than it is to run a financially unsuccessful design studio.

Everything else about running a studio I learned from a book called *The Business of Graphic Design*. A pragmatic business book giving the reasons why you should or shouldn't start your own company, it talked about how to design a business plan and estimate overheads. It described the advantages of both setting up alone and of partnerships.

I was also influenced by Quentin Crisp, now—sadly—remembered mainly as the subject of Sting's song "An Englishman in New York." He talked to one of my classes, and he was such an inspiring character. Among the many smart things he said was: "Everybody who tells the truth is interesting." So I thought: this is easy, just try to be open and forthright and it will be interesting.

I recently took a year off from clients. I used the time to make up my mind about all the fields I did not want to get into (but had previously imagined I would). I surprised myself by getting up every day at 6am to conduct little type experiments (without a looming deadline). It made me think a lot about clients. I decided that I would rather have an educated client than one I have to educate. Tibor's line was that he would only take on clients smarter than him (but remember, a client does not have to be design literate to be smart). After reopening, I also decided to widen the scope of our studio to include four distinct areas: design for social causes, design for artists, corporate design, and design for music.

So how does a graphic designer avoid losing his or her soul? Having misplaced little pieces of mine, I'm not sure if I am the right person to answer this question. What soul I have left I've managed to keep by pausing; by stopping and thinking. In my regular day-to-day mode, I get so caught up in the minutiae that I have little time or sense to think about the larger context. Because I used to work in different cities, a natural gap occurred between jobs, allowing for some reflection. When I got tired of moving and decided to stay put in New York, I created those gaps artificially by taking my year off or by teaching for a semester in Berlin. But even three days out of the office, alone, in a foreign city can do the trick.

I hope this book helps young designers find their way. I don't think that the "designers don't read" bullshit is true. A good book will find good readers.

## How to be a graphic designer, without losing your soul

To paraphrase Frank Zappa: here's just what the world needs—another graphic design book. Graphic design books are nearly as common as celebrity diet books or airport blockbusters. But for the committed designer there are few better ways to spend an hour than immersed in the pages of a toothsome design book—we enjoy the bug-eyed envy that comes from looking at work we wish we'd done ourselves, and we are inspired by the dizzying range of graphic expression on view. And of course, as much as we enjoy the work, we also like to find fault with it. Moaning is important to designers; it's something we do well. But although design books can sometimes be accused of contributing to the widely held misconception that design is an effortless activity practiced by star designers who never break sweat as they glide from triumph to triumph, they are, on the whole, *a good thing.*

Stefan Sagmeister's book *Made You Look* is one of the few design books that attempts to show a warts-and-all picture of the working life of a designer. He reproduces his failures ("the bad stuff") as well as his triumphs, he itemizes the fees he received, and in a pictorial cartoon reveals that even superstar designers have their work tampered with by meddlesome clients.

And yet there's something missing in this encyclopedic coverage of design. When we gorge ourselves on the succulent work in the books, and when we slurp through the numerous magazines and web sites that chronicle the design scene, we rarely get the back-story; we rarely get the grubby bits that go with almost every job. Designers are quick to tell us about their sources of inspiration ("I'm really into Otl Aicher's pictograms and I like this beet-flavored chewing-gum wrapper I brought back from Osaka"), but they are much less willing to reveal tiresome matters such as how they find clients, how much they charge, and what they do when their client rejects three weeks of work and refuses to pay the bill.[1] If you want to learn how to be a designer, you need to know about these and other messy matters. It's as much a part of being a designer as knowing how to kern type or design the perfect letterhead. In fact, how you deal with the grubby bits is how you learn to be a graphic designer.

This is a book written by a designer *for* designers. It combines practical advice and philosophical guidance to help the independent-minded graphic designer deal with the knottier problems encountered by the working designer. I've added the phrase "without losing your soul" to the book's title because it seemed the best way to emphasize a key aspect of my intention: namely, to write a book designed to help those who believe that graphic design has a cultural and aesthetic value beyond the mere trumpeting of commercial messages; a book for those who believe that we become graphic designers because we are attracted to the act of personal creation; and a book for those who believe that design is at its best when the designer's voice is allowed to register, and is not suppressed in favor of blandness and sameness.

This book is also a response to the fact that more people than ever are studying and practising graphic design. Where once it was seen as a purely artisanal occupation with not much status attached to it, it is now regarded as a meaningful, even mildly glamorous activity. Today, you can say that you are a graphic designer without people looking at you as if you've just announced that you do nude salsa dancing. Fashion designers, architects, and product designers are already part of the new cultural elite: Tom Ford, Frank Gehry, and Jonathan Ive are frequently interviewed with breathless reverence in newspapers, magazines, and on television. And although graphic designers are not yet regarded with such slack-jawed wonder, David Carson, Peter Saville, Stefan Sagmeister, Neville Brody, and a few others have a star rating that lifts them into the lower reaches of the celebrity designer cosmos.

According to a recent US Department of Labor report,[2] there are 532,000 designers employed in the United States; 212,000 of these are graphic designers. In her book, *The Substance of Style*, Virginia Postrel points out that at least fifty graphic design magazines are regularly published around the world (there were three in 1970); and she quotes Pentagram partner and noted design commentator Michael Bierut: "There's no such thing as an un-designed graphic object anymore, and there used to be."

However, despite all this graphic abundance, most of the design that surrounds us lacks emotional character or aesthetic value. It's just there; clogging up the arteries of our visual lives. As the designer Paula Scher (also of Pentagram), noted in a 1994 essay published in the *AIGA Journal*: "Everyday I find myself in supermarkets, discount drugstores, video shops, and other environments that are obviously untouched by our community … just plain old-fashioned non-controversial bad design, the kind of anonymous bad design that we've come to ignore because we're too busy fighting over the aesthetics of the latest AIGA poster."[3] The prevalence of "bad design" is a consequence of an increasingly competitive and globalized economy, where risk is anathema, where the herd instinct predominates, and where sameness is the default position. It is unthinkable today that a powerful global brand would employ a contemporary designer in the way that IBM once employed Paul Rand, or that a commercial magazine sold on the newsstands would grant the freedom *The Face* gave Neville Brody in the 1980s. Focus groups and marketing imperatives would smother such initiatives at birth.

Design itself is now intensely competitive; so much so, in fact, that many designers have become browbeaten into timidity and compliance. This is hardly surprising, since it's hard to take a stand on matters of principle when there are countless other firms and individuals willing to do the work if you don't. But, hang on, what's so bad about giving clients what they want? Isn't design a service industry?

This takes us to the heart of one of the most important debates in design over recent years. On the one hand, we have those who believe that graphic design is a problem-solving, business tool and that designers should suppress their desire for personal expression to ensure maximizing the effectiveness of the content. While on the other hand, we have those who believe that although design undoubtedly has a problem-solving function, it also has a cultural and aesthetic dimension, and its effectiveness is enhanced, and not diminished, by personal expression.

2   This report, among others, can be found at bls.gov/oco/ocos090.stm

3   "The Devaluation of Design by the Design Community," *AIGA Journal*, New York, 1994. Reprinted in Robyn Marsack, *Essays on Design 1: AGI's Designers of Influence* (London: Booth-Clibborn Editions), 1997.

## How to be a graphic designer, without losing your soul

The former remains the dominant view among professional designers. But this traditionalist view of graphic design has always been subjected to critical attack and scepticism by radical voices in design, especially since the anti-globalization movement threw down a challenge to corporate behemoths in the late 1990s. And this pragmatic view of the designer's role doesn't hold true in other areas of design: we don't ask architects or fashion designers to suppress their personal voices–quite the opposite. In fact, we value most those who are capable of investing their work with personal statements. Nor, paradoxically, does the pragmatic view seem to have a basis in commercial reality. Increasingly, the messages that get noticed are the ones where the designer's thumbprint is clearly visible: the ones that contain a rebel yell of defiance.

Nor is this schism as simple as a mere divergence between conservatives and radicals. If you read the design press you might think that the desire for creative freedom, or self-expression, was confined to superstar designers: it's not, it's actually universal. We become graphic designers because we want to say something. We want to make a visual statement for which we can stake a claim for authorship; in some cases it is a very modest claim, but it's a claim nonetheless. And even for those designers who fervently subscribe to the notion that the designer's contribution is always subservient to the client's needs and wishes, these individuals still want to perform this function their way. Let me put it another way: I don't think I've ever met a designer who didn't have the instinct for self-expression. You can see it in the universal reluctance to have ideas rejected, tampered with, or watered down. There's a mule-like instinct in nearly every designer–even the most accommodating and service-minded–that bristles at the command "Oh, can you change that" and the "Just do it like this" attitude so frequently adopted by design's paymasters–the clients. It's an instinct, inherent in all designers, that says: a little bit of my soul has gone into this and it is not going to be removed without a fight.

The situation is further complicated by the fact that all graphic designers agree that there are, unquestionably, purely practical and utilitarian roles for graphic design. Applications such as road signs, medicine packaging, timetables, and the presentation of financial, scientific, or technical data, require design of the utmost clarity and precision. It is broadly agreed that there is no room in this sphere for notions such as personal expression or experimentation. A badly designed road sign might kill you: death by typography is a real possibility. And yet, show me a designer who doesn't want to execute even these tasks in the way he or she sees fit?

To arrive at a definition of what this book will tell you, it might be easier to say what this book will *not* tell you. This book will not tell you how to work the trapping functions in QuarkXPress. It will not tell you anything about hardware, software, or the minutiae of Apple's latest operating system. There are countless books on these subjects, and in my experience designers learn these skills only when they need to, and they learn them from other designers or by working them out for themselves.

This book doesn't tell you what sort of designer you should be. In matters of styles, trends, and schools of design, this book is agnostic. It will not tell you what typefaces are cool nor what the current trends in layout, photography, and illustration are. It will not advocate the supremacy of formal design over vernacular design, or the desirability of Helvetica over Bodoni. You can get this information by looking at books and magazines, by reading about graphic design history, by talking to other designers, and by experimentation within your own work. And although the great Josef Müller-Brockmann said "All design work has a political character,"[4] this book assumes that political questions are a matter for individual consciences. If, for instance, you are asked to design the packaging for a canned drink which contains dubious chemicals, you have a moral decision to make. Your conscience might tell you not to do this work, but if you are struggling to pay your bills you will find it hard to say no. This book doesn't tell you what to do in this situation: only you can make the decision.

Nor does this book tell you how to file your tax returns, prepare management accounts, or deal with the complexities of employment law. There are much better equipped writers than me to tell you these things (a bibliography and appendix are provided at the back of this book), and in my experience, designers are, as a rule, not interested in this sort of information and also not very good at absorbing it until they have to. However, if you are going to survive—either as a freelance designer or by running a small studio—you are going to have to know about these things. So, rather than tell you how to do these things, I am going to tell you how to find accountants and other professional advisers to do them for you.[5]

I think the reader is now entitled to ask, well, what *does* this book tell me about? It gives the answers to some questions that designers ask themselves repeatedly. The urge to write this volume came from speaking to—and more importantly, listening to—students and young working designers. As a frequent visitor to design colleges, I am asked questions such as: "How do you respond to crap briefs?"; "How do you stop clients demanding unreasonable changes to your work?"; "How do you find interesting work?" I hear similar questions when I talk to designers who've been in practice for two or three years: "How do you do good work and make money?"; "How do you stop clients changing your work?"; "How do you avoid spending your whole life doing unpaid pitches for low-budget work?"

It occurred to me that here was a stratum of questions—a mixture of the practical and the philosophical—that graphic designers found hard to get answers to. The art schools are preoccupied with producing "broadly based" graduates and have insufficient time to prepare students for every aspect of working life. The glossy design press devotes its energies to chronicling the work of the latest hot designers, but avoids the practical issues facing working designers. Design writing and critical discourse rarely touch on the practicalities of life as a designer.[6] And as more and more designers emerge from higher education only to be faced with the realization that there are not enough jobs to go round, they are having to acquire levels of entrepreneurial determination that previous generations didn't need until much later in their careers. "How to be a graphic designer …" sets out to fill some of these gaps and offers advice and guidance that suit the sensibilities of independent-minded designers.

4 Interview in *Eye* 19, winter 1995.

5 In America, the aptly named *How* magazine covers practical issues relating to professional practice, with many useful articles on the less glamorous aspects of life as a designer, often written by practicing designers. In the UK, *Design Week*, which claims to be the world's only weekly design magazine, regularly devotes space to practical matters.

6 The US writer and designer Kenneth Fitzgerald touched on this subject in an *Eye* magazine article titled "Fanfare for the Common Hack" (*Eye* 27, spring 1998), in which he urged theorists not to turn a deaf ear to "down-in-the-trenches" designers.

**How to be a graphic designer, without losing your soul**

So who is this book aimed at? You might say that this is a book for designers who accept design's conventional role, but who also see a parallel role for design as a culturally and socially beneficial force. If you want to narrow the book's focus still further, I'd say it is a practical and philosophical guide for students emerging, or about to emerge, from higher education and for working designers in the early stages of their careers. It is first and foremost a book for the free-thinking designer.

But who am I to tell you about these matters? I am a self-taught graphic designer. I started out as a trainee in a big studio in the pre-digital era. I was informally apprenticed to a group of experienced designers who taught me the basics of typography, showed me how to prepare mechanical artwork, gave me a CMYK color percentages chart, and left me to get on with it. This was daunting, but it was also my lucky break. I'd been a bit of a wastrel up until this point. But within a few weeks I was producing acceptable commercial design and artwork, and as a reward I was given a full-time job as a junior designer. You could say that graphic design saved my life.

Until recently I was creative director of a design company called Intro. I co-founded the company in 1988 with my then business partner Katy Richardson. We won awards and built up a small but steadily growing reputation in the UK and overseas, as a reliable, well-run, and inventive design company. Our clients were an assortment of record labels, blue-chip corporations, arts organizations, educational bodies, and media companies; we even had the British National Health Service as a client and managed to produce effective work for them, while also working for bands like Primal Scream and Stereolab. We were early proponents of the new cross-media approach to graphic design; we were among the first companies in the digital era to combine design and film-making (digital and traditional) under the same roof, something that has become more common since.

As the company grew (we were forty-strong at one giddy point) I did less and less design. As creative director, I was involved in finding and developing young designers, and acting as the bridge between our designers and our clients. I discovered a talent for advocacy, and I learned that communication skills are one of the most valuable abilities a designer can have. In December 2003 I left Intro and set up as a freelance art director, writer, and consultant. At Intro we came as close as is possible in a tough and unforgiving world to being a profitable (although not rich) design company that also did groundbreaking work. Our combination of creativity underpinned by business rigor worked well; but it was hard graft, and after fifteen years I began to feel the strain. Intro continues to prosper and do excellent work.

The book also contains contributions from leading designers. In a series of interviews they reveal their approaches to common problems faced by young designers making decisions early in their careers.

A final word before we start: you can ignore every piece of advice contained in these pages and still become a successful and fulfilled designer. All my advice comes with an override button: there is no such thing as a set of rules that will turn you into the complete graphic designer. In my vision of how to be a graphic designer there is always room for the maverick, the difficult, and the downright contrary. I'm not trying to create homogenized designers. Far from it: what I want to do is provide the reader with a series of clues, hints, and prompts to help make working life more enjoyable and rewarding. I want to talk about subjects that are not often discussed, and matters that are "assumed" to be understood, but which rarely are. I want to help you avoid making the mistakes that I made. I want to help you become an effective and self-reliant graphic designer—without losing your soul along the way.

Attributes needed by the modern designer Cultural awareness / communication / integrity
A discussion about the key attributes required by the contemporary graphic designer. Or how to prevent your work being mangled by irate clients.

**How to be a graphic designer, without losing your soul**

What are the essential qualities needed to be a graphic designer? There was a time when all we needed to earn a living and call ourselves a designer was talent and mastery of a few craft skills. Today we need more. The modern designer needs to be a diplomat, a business thinker, a researcher, an aesthete, an ethicist, an innovator—in fact, a polymath. And yet, it seems to me that all the necessary qualities to be a designer can be boiled down to three essential attributes that we need to combine with talent and craft skills: cultural awareness, communication skills, and integrity. They may sound grandiose and intimidating but, as we shall see, they are really everyday qualities that many designers possess naturally, and that others acquire over time, through hard work and dedication.

## Cultural awareness

There are thousands of definitions of graphic design. Here's one that really hits a vein, by the American designer and writer Jessica Helfand: "Graphic design is a visual language uniting harmony and balance, color and light, scale and tension, form and content. But it is also an idiomatic language, a language of cues and puns and symbols and allusions, of cultural references and perceptual inferences that challenge both the intellect and the eye."[1]

Helfand's first sentence is a conventional summary of graphic design; few would argue with it. But her next sentence is a blockbuster. It alludes to design's power to evoke emotion and generate an intellectual response. Cues, puns, symbols, allusions, cultural references, and perceptual inferences are the essential elements that give authority and resonance to visual design work. The only way we can introduce these qualities into our work is by taking a tireless interest in everything that goes on around us. In other words, we must develop an insatiable curiosity about areas other than graphic design—politics, entertainment, business, technology, art, ten-pin bowling, and mud wrestling.

[1] Quoted by Virginia Postrel in *The Substance of Style*, New York, HarperCollins, 2003.

Hang on. Cultural awareness? Surely this is just old-fashioned research? Surely every designer knows that when we start a new project we have to do some mental (or actual) legwork and swot up on the subject. This is true; research is a vital part of being a designer. I once turned up for a meeting with some people from an art gallery who were looking for a new design company. Arrogantly, I didn't do any research. I relied on a shaky notion of who I thought my potential client was, when in fact, I'd mixed them up with another gallery. My mistake was exposed and I got a frosty response. Needless to say, I didn't get the gig.

By cultural awareness I mean something deeper and more wide-ranging than research. When the British writer Iain Sinclair was asked if he did research for his books, he replied that *his whole life was research*. I can't think of a better motto for the modern graphic designer. Without constantly scanning, scrutinizing, and absorbing everything that goes on around us, we can't hope to become successful and effective designers.

The graphic designer and typographer Erik Spiekermann has employed dozens—perhaps hundreds—of designers in his career. In an interview I asked him what he looked for in a candidate:

"…they have to have general knowledge. I hate people who don't read. I hate people who don't cook, or don't know anything about music. I couldn't work with anyone who only goes to McDonalds. I want people who know movies, who know music, who read books. As you know, not all graphic designers are 'multi-dimensional.' They don't read, they don't do anything else, and I couldn't work with those people. I need team people who have general knowledge because that's what we do…"[2]

2  Adrian Shaughnessy and Tony Brook, *Studio Culture*, Unit Editions, 2009.

I once read that safe-crackers rubbed the tips of their fingers with sandpaper to increase tactile sensitivity. It makes them ultra-sensitive and enables them to feel the nuances of the lock's mechanism as they rotate the dial in search of the magic combination that will open the safe. It's the same with graphic design: we need to find ways to make us more sensitive to the world around us.

Designers sometimes imagine that the world revolves around graphic design. And when we are working fourteen-hour days and thinking about design problems from the moment we wake till the moment we go to sleep, it's hard to remember that there are other things in the world besides typefaces, colors, and paper stocks. But the best designers are always characterized by an interest in life beyond their subject; design is their main concern, and it provides them with a consuming and stimulating career, but it doesn't eclipse other interests.[3]

Non-designers often accuse graphic designers of being nerds who are only interested in ourselves and our work. This is a pretty damning appraisal, since the single most important thing a designer can do when discussing a project with a new or potential client is to demonstrate understanding of the subject under discussion and show knowledge of the way the world works and the way people think and act. The designer who shows only signs of self-absorption and narrow focus is not going to inspire his or her client.

The designer Lorraine Wild describes the benefits of understanding the "larger context" in which her work is situated: "I used to do more research and now I'm more intuitive. I've gotten better at understanding the materials that I'm given to work with by writers, editors, curators, artists and architects, etc. I have always been conscientious about knowing the material, but now I've accumulated a library in my head which helps me read the larger context that surrounds the subject I'm about to work with…" "Reputations," *Eye* 36, summer 2000.

However, many designers use encounters with clients as opportunities to talk about themselves and boast about their skills and achievements. These are often the same designers who complain that their work is frequently rejected or that they are never allowed to "do what they want to do." This is hardly surprising. They are guilty of the worst crime a graphic designer can commit: they are revealing themselves to be self-centered and to have a limited outlook. For the ambitious designer, this is fatal. To counter this understandable instinct for self-promotion I have a rule when meeting clients: I never talk about myself until they ask me to. Instead, I let them talk, I ask them questions about their business, and I allow them to have center stage. Then, a little bit of magic occurs; they (usually) turn to me and say—*OK, tell me about you.*

**How to be a graphic designer, without losing your soul**

Of course, there's a paradox here: to be good designers we have to be utterly dedicated to our chosen career, yet our dedication is often mistaken by clients as self-centered obsessiveness and makes them think we are unreceptive toward their needs. However, if we can talk about the project at hand; if we can show that we understand the cultural or business context into which their project fits; and if we can listen instead of prattling on about ourselves, we will find our clients more receptive to our ideas and willing to take us seriously. It's another paradox, but the less we make a client/designer relationship about ourselves the more it will tip in our favor.

## Communication

As well as keeping our surveillance cameras pointed at the world beyond graphic design, the modern designer needs to be a skilled communicator. This doesn't mean making eloquent speeches at design conferences, or delivering blockbuster presentations to boardrooms full of marketing executives. What we're discussing here is the ability to speak about our work to clients and non-designers in a coherent, convincing, and objective way without resorting to the language and idioms that we might use when talking to other designers. And since communication is a two-way street, it is also about listening. An inability to listen is a serious handicap for a designer—it's like trying to sprint while wearing full scuba-diving kit.

But why this emphasis on talking about our work? Surely the point of graphic design is that it speaks for itself? Well, it's true that graphic communication is required to function without the benefit of written or spoken commentaries describing the designer's intentions: we can't stand in the street beside a poster we've designed and draw the attention of passersby to our subtle use of Akzidenz Grotesk, with its mute evocation of Modernist rationality and truthfulness. Yet there never was a client who didn't demand to know why we've done what we've shown them. If we can't explain our decisions in a convincing and objective way, we risk rejection and failure. As Norman Potter notes in his seminal text *What is a Designer*: "This aspect of design work is frequently underestimated: an ability to use words clearly, pointedly, and persuasively is at all times relevant to design work."[4]

4   Norman Potter, *What is a Designer*, London, Hyphen Press, 2002.

Persuading clients that our ideas are good, and that their money is being spent wisely, requires carefully formulated arguments combined with lots of stamina and determination. But for many designers, this requirement is a source of lip-chewing frustration. All good designers focus their efforts on their target audience, yet are compelled to spend almost as much time and energy persuading clients to back their ideas. This is one of the inescapable facts of life for the modern graphic designer: we always have gatekeepers (clients) standing between us and our intended audiences (end users, or human beings as I prefer to call them).

This is why the way in which we present our ideas is as important as the ideas them-selves. When a good idea is rejected, it's often the presentation of that idea that is being rejected, not the idea itself. So far I've talked a great deal about clients. But really I'm talking about anyone who we have to make presentations to. And no matter where we find ourselves in the graphic design landscape, we always have to make presentations. Designers who work in corporations or small businesses often report to non-designers; junior designers in design studios are required to present work to creative directors, team leaders, or senior designers. These people are "clients," and how we treat them determines how they treat our work. For the ambitious designer, being good at presenting work is as important as having a head for heights for a high-wire walker.

However, considering the importance of presenting our work, it's surprising to dis-cover that we designers are often not much good at it. In Chapter 2 I discuss the finer points of making a presentation (think of it as the graphic designer's equivalent of the Japanese tea ceremony), but for now I'll just make the point that knowing how to talk about our work, how to explain it, and how to present it, is fundamental to becoming a well-rounded designer.

To help young designers develop the verbal skills they need to talk about their work I sometimes ask them *not* to show me what they've done but to describe the work instead. I do this to encourage them to talk about their work with objectivity and passion. I know experienced designers who can persuade clients to sign off complex (and expensive) projects purely on their ability to talk compellingly about their ideas. I've also seen resourceful designers rescue disas-trous presentations by coming up with instant ideas and describing them in vivid and simple language. I don't recommend verbal presentations as an alternative to showing mock-ups; cli-ents always want to see what they are buying. But the ability to describe our ideas is an essential component of any presentation. Any designer who thinks it's enough to throw work on the table and say nothing will soon be stacking shelves in the local supermarket rather than designing the packaging that sits on those shelves.

As I've already mentioned, communication is a two-way street. This means that no matter how good we are at talking about our work, we must also remember to listen. The reason for this would become instantly clear to any designer nimble enough to climb inside the heads of one of their clients: they'd discover someone fretting about spending money on something that he or she can't see or touch. Think of it like this: imagine going into a chic furniture store and telling the sales assistant that you'd like to buy a sofa. "Sure," she says, "we've got lots of won-derful sofas. I can sell you one—but I can't let you see it." If this happened you'd walk out and go to a furniture store where you could see what you were buying; at the very least, you'd want to check the color and sink yourself into the upholstery. Yet when clients buy design, especially from a new and untried graphic designer, they don't know what they are buying until it is deliv-ered. This aspect of design leads to more unhappiness and failed projects than any other factor in the relationships between designers and their clients. But by listening intently and identifying the factors that worry our clients, we can help to make the commissioning process, the presen-tation process, and the creative process far less of a gamble for our clients.

**How to be a graphic designer, without losing your soul**

Before we go much further, I need to say here that I'm assuming that the readers of this book are designers who have a point of view—or, to put it another way, designers who don't see themselves as doormats. Doormat designers are people who take the view that design is about giving clients exactly what they want. There is nothing wrong with this; there is plenty of work for anyone who gives their clients whatever they want with no arguments, no questioning of briefs, and no rocking of the boat. But, for designers who want to produce work that has depth and resonance, being a doormat designer isn't an option. So, assuming that I'm talking to designers with a viewpoint, and assuming that I'm talking to designers who want to find a way of expressing their viewpoints, we arrive at the most important aspect of communication between designer and client: clients will take our opinions seriously only if we give their opinions the same value. In other words, there has to be a balance of interests. All great work comes about when viewpoints are balanced; when both client and designer feel that they are being listened to and that their views are respected. When we find that point of balance in a relationship, we hit gold.

This brings us to the central conundrum at the heart of graphic design: the conflict between inner conviction and the need for external rationality. What does this mean? It means that we become graphic designers because we discover that we have an aptitude and a compulsion for what Jessica Helfand calls "uniting harmony and balance, color and light, scale and tension, form and content." To complicate the matter still further, we also discover that we have something called creative intuition, for which we can't always offer a rational explanation, but which is nevertheless a tangible and vital part of our life as a creative producer. In practice, this means that we use fonts, colors, layouts, and imagery because of an inner aesthetic conviction—and when you think about it, it would be an odd designer who used elements that he or she didn't like. Even when designers are being totally subservient to the brief, they still use styles and modes of expression that they are personally convinced are right. And here's where the conundrum kicks in: we have to learn to present these "inner convictions," these "intuitions" as rational and objective.

The designer Rudy VanderLans identified this problem when he wrote: "You have to listen very carefully to what the client wants and be careful not to approach the project with a preconceived idea of what it should look like. In my own experience, too often I approached a design job wanting to use a certain font or a particular typographic mannerism, simply because it's what I felt comfortable with at the time. But that wasn't always what the client wanted."

This is a hot potato for all designers—even for the most pragmatic and service-minded. Few clients will accept the argument "I've done it like this because I like it," yet this is often what we've done. But if we want to see our ideas come to fruition, we have to dress them up in the objective language that clients understand. It's a subject that the designer Michael Bierut has dealt with in an influential blog post on Design Observer called "On (Design) Bullshit." He wrote: "It follows that every design presentation is inevitably, at least in part, an exercise in bullshit. The design process always combines the pursuit of functional goals with countless intuitive, even irrational decisions. The functional requirements—the house needs a bathroom, the headlines have to be legible, the toothbrush has to fit in your mouth—are concrete and often measurable. The intuitive decisions, on the other hand, are more or less beyond honest explanation. These might be: I just like to set my headlines in Bodoni, or I just like to make my products blobby, or I just like to cover my buildings in gridded white porcelain panels. In discussing design work with their clients, designers are direct about the functional parts of their solutions and obfuscate like mad about the intuitive parts, having learned early on that telling the simple truth—'I don't know, I just like it that way'—simply won't do."

In lectures and talks when I've discussed the subject of disguising or obfuscating personal convictions and intuition, I've been accused of promoting hypocrisy and dishonesty. The charge sticks. I'd like not to have to put a spin on what I do, and my aim in all client relationships is to quickly get to a point where it is possible to be frank with them, and in turn, for them to give honest appraisals and reactions. But until that point is reached—the point of balance that I mentioned earlier—we have to indulge in a ritual dance that everyone knows is bullshit, but that few of us feel able to dispense with. To me, the role of bullshit in design is a bit like good manners in daily life: if we always say what we think, we end up offending everyone we come into contact with. Instead, we develop codes by which we allow each other to coexist without the need to punch each other at every utterance.

A last word on communication: our clients are not the only people we have to communicate with effectively. If we have designers as partners, or if we employ designers, we have to be able to communicate with them in such a way that they feel inspired and encouraged. We also have to be able to talk to suppliers and collaborators, not to mention IT people, bank managers, tax officials, and window cleaners.

## Integrity

After extolling the virtues of bullshit, it seems strange to now extol the virtues of integrity. So what does integrity mean in design? Does it mean being true to ourselves and standing up for what we believe in? Does it mean behaving professionally at all times toward our clients? Or is it about doing the best we can on behalf of our intended audience? Well, it means all of these things. Yet there's no denying that preserving our integrity in the remorseless climate of modern business is not easy. Integrity often becomes a bargaining chip. We give it away in return for a job that comes with a lot of cash, or we hang onto it in order to do the work we want to do, often for little or no money. It is tough to retain integrity and make a living. But it's not impossible.

As designers, we are free to conduct ourselves in any way we want. Specific offences such as copyright infringement and software theft are punishable in law, but unlike lawyers and real estate agents, designers don't have codes of conduct, and we are as free as the marketplace allows us to be.

I've always relished this freedom, but in recent years I've come to question it. I now hold the view that designers, and design itself, would benefit from an ethical code. This is not just my view; I see a hunger for ethical guidelines expressed in design blogs and by the rise of interest in design with a social focus. I also see it in the students I talk to who are keen to do work with an ethical focus. I've also noticed that, as a general rule, designers who behave ethically don't suffer in the way they might once have done. Take those studios that advocate a green approach to design; there was a time when they might have struggled to attract clients, but now they are seen as an attractive option for the many clients who want to work sustainably. The same is true of studios that operate ethical codes relating to the sort of work they will and won't do; at one time they might have been avoided, but today they are sought out by the many bodies and institutions that have their own ethical requirements and standards.

**How to be a graphic designer, without losing your soul**

Professional design associations have made attempts in the past to draw up ethical codes, but they have tended to be undermined by shifts in public and business morality, or overtaken by rapid technological change. In the 1971 edition of her book *The Professional Practice of Design*, the British writer Dorothy Goslett wrote about the codes of conduct advocated by SIAD (Society of Industrial Artists and Designers, now called the Chartered Society of Designers). She notes that one of the rules states: "A member (of the SIAD) shall not knowingly accept any professional assignment on which another designer has been or is working except with the agreement of the other designer or until he is satisfied that the former appointment has been properly terminated."

In today's market economy, where willingness to indulge in the competitive "belittling" of our rivals is legitimized and encouraged by governments and business leaders, the SIAD's prohibition on poaching clients seems touchingly outmoded. But is it? I was talking to a designer friend recently and I mentioned that I'd heard on the grapevine that a large upmarket retailer in central London—a world-famous name—was looking for new designers to commission. My friend thanked me for the tip-off, but said that he couldn't approach the retailer because a designer friend of his already worked for them. I was struck by his old-fashioned loyalty. It's what I mean when I talk about integrity; a personal philosophy that is not abandoned at the first sign of personal gain.

Of course, there are lots of ways of having integrity. At its most earthbound, integrity might be as simple as a love of design expressed in such a way that clients can see that it is something more than professional expediency. Alternatively, it might take a more practical form; it might be a refusal to take part in "free pitches." Free—or unpaid—pitching, is a hotly debated issue in contemporary design. Very few jobs of any size are assigned without a competitive pitch, and frequently these pitches are unpaid. In an era of transparency in financial reporting, and new tendering rules in Europe, nearly all public bodies (and many private firms) are obliged to offer contracts up to open tender as a way of avoiding corruption, nepotism, and favoritism.

Whenever designers gather to discuss their work, the subject of free pitching arises; various professional bodies around the world have tried to formulate a correct response to this practice, but without much success. It is now so prevalent that it is almost impossible to avoid if you want to be in contention for many of the plum jobs that are offered to designers. Yet free pitching obstructs one of the fundamental ways in which good work is achieved; for good work to emerge, designers and clients must form a partnership and explore all avenues together in a mutually trusting and open way. This is rarely possible in a competitive pitch. No matter how good the brief, the designer is not able to interrogate the client in the way that a client would be interrogated in a proper commission: the designer is merely taking part in a beauty parade, or more, a lottery.

When we make this argument to clients, some of the smarter ones can see the merit in our case, but most see only the substantial benefit they derive—at zero cost—from being presented with a range of free responses to their brief that helps them to make and justify their final choice (they have something to evaluate it against). In other words, clients are receiving a quantifiable benefit that they do not pay for. Despite the widespread dislike of unpaid pitching among designers, there is not much chance of the practice becoming any less common; in fact, the opposite is happening, with even small projects being offered up for pitch. Laudable as it is to encourage fairness in commissioning, designers who are expected to produce creative work without payment seem unduly penalized by this new drive for fiscal transparency.

But here's a funny thing: there are many studios and individuals who take a principled stance and say no to free pitching and, perhaps surprisingly, they seem to survive pretty well. The English designer Jonathan Ellery runs the design company Browns. He makes the following statement on the homepage of the group's web site: WE DON'T LIKE SAYING NO, SO PLEASE DON'T ASK US TO FREE PITCH OR WORK FOR UNETHICAL CAUSES.[5]

Are Browns damaged by this statement? Not at all. Instead they are seen as dignified and principled, and continue to attract high-quality clients. So, could it be that by standing up for what we believe in, studios actually grow rather than diminish in stature? It certainly appears to be the case that designers who believe in nothing only ever attract clients who don't believe in them.

This was true of my early days as a designer: when I started out, I was so keen to please my clients and employers that I avoided having any opinions and told them only what I thought they wanted to hear. In other words, I demonstrated the morals of the marketplace and consequently was treated like a commodity: my services were bought at bargain-basement prices and my opinions rarely valued. And here's another funny thing: in a world with no principles, people often most respect those who have principles.

It is not just in our work that we need to display integrity. We must have integrity in the way we deal with other designers, with our suppliers (printers, web programmers, technicians), and with people we meet in professional life (everybody from office cleaners to bank managers). We must also have integrity in the way we handle the creative work of other designers, of photographers, and of illustrators. Many of us will have been cavalier at some point in our working lives and used typefaces, photographs, or graphics software that we didn't pay for—but this is theft as surely as if we'd gone into someone's house and taken their possessions. Most important of all, we have to show integrity to the three "audiences" for which nearly all design is created: our clients, our intended audience, and ourselves. Designers will differ on the order of importance in which they place this trinity and in my view, if we want to produce meaningful work, the demands and responsibilities of all three have to be equally balanced.[6]

[5] Our policy at Intro was to participate in unpaid pitches if they opened doors that would otherwise remain closed to us. Because we weren't a conventional design group, we were often added to a pitch list as a wildcard entry, so the client could demonstrate that they had asked a variety of studios to compete. We used these opportunities to good advantage, often winning jobs by doing our homework as thoroughly as the others but also by bringing freshness to what was new territory for us, and thereby exposing the formulaic nature of our more sector-experienced competitors. But, before agreeing to free pitch, we always asked for a pitch fee (sometimes, to our surprise, we got one; sometimes we didn't). We insisted on knowing who we were pitching against and we made a friendly protest (through gritted teeth) about the inadvisability of pitches being the best way to commission design.

[6] Peter Saville told The Times of London (15 September 2004): "The trouble with graphic design today is: when can you believe it? It's not the message of the designer anymore. Every applied artist ends up selling his or her soul at some point. I haven't done it and look at me. People call me one of the most famous designers in the world and I haven't got any money."

**How to be a graphic designer, without losing your soul**

By standing up for ourselves, by having beliefs (creative and ethical), and by questioning what we are asked to do as designers, we can acquire self-respect, and self-respect is the first step on the path to earning the respect of clients and other designers. We might also get the sack, or incur the wrath of our clients, but that's integrity for you—there's a price to be paid for it. Just remember, it's always less than the price of our self-respect.

## Conclusion

So far, I've only dealt with some rather grand notions about how to be a graphic designer. In subsequent chapters I'll tackle more mundane matters such as how to find a job, how to prepare a portfolio, and how to have good ideas. Yet without the attributes of cultural awareness, communication skills, and professional and personal integrity, you won't grow as a designer. Some designers are born with all the qualities they need; the rest of us have to work to acquire them. This takes time, and there will be disappointments and setbacks along the way.

Investigation of the key "hard" and "soft" skills required by the modern designer. Or the non-designing part of being a graphic designer.

# How to be a graphic designer, without losing your soul

In the previous chapter I listed the three essential attributes that the modern graphic designer needs to be a fully functioning practitioner: cultural awareness, communication skills, and integrity. You might call these *attitudes of mind*. They are qualities that cannot be learned from a manual. They are acquired by living and doing, and thinking about how we live and do.

Yet even when a designer can boast that he or she possesses this trio of attributes, there are at least another two levels of capabilities that are needed.

The first of these two levels is practical skills. These include every technical and manual skill required by designers to perform their jobs. I'm thinking of software prowess; technical knowledge of printing, coding, or color theory, and the presentation of information in a usable, attractive, and logical way. These skills can be taught, although they are best developed heuristically—in other words, we can be taught the basics, but we only expand our capabilities by doing. No amount of reading or instruction will enable us to lay out a page of text as effectively as the lessons we learn from physically doing it. It's what makes graphic design different from most other professions (and why it is often treated with suspicion by non-designers).[1]

In this chapter, we are concerned with the third level; what the designer Michael Bierut calls the *non-designing bit of being a designer*.

[1] With his customary lowercase perceptivity, the great German designer Otl Aicher noted: "Graphic design is one of the last free professions that is not forced into the corset of a career structure and thus inhibited by standards and guidelines. There is no career structure upon which the state could accompany designers with examinations and checks, and of course also with certificates and prizes, with awards and titles. A graphic designer is a graphic designer." Taken from *otl aicher, the world as design*, Wiley-VCH, 1994.

## Time management

If clients butchering work is the favorite gripe of designers, then never having enough time to do a job properly must come second. No matter how much time we have for a project, it's never enough. Even when a thoughtful client or a considerate employer gives us a generous lump of time, what do we do with it? We delay starting the project until the last possible moment, then end up doing the task in the same amount of time we would have had if we'd been given the usual "want-it-tomorrow" schedule. And who in the history of graphic design ever made a presentation that wasn't finished minutes before the presentation was due to be made? Not me, that's for sure.

Yet it is an illusion to imagine that we never have enough time. What we really mean when we say that we don't have enough time is that *we have a problem managing our time*. This is understandable. As creative people working in a commercial environment, we are dependent on a myriad of factors, many of them outside our direct control. I'm thinking about poor or constantly changing briefs; late copy and frequent alterations to project specifications; and the unavailability of collaborators or suppliers (graphic designers rarely work in isolation—our activities nearly always have to dovetail with others, and these "others" aren't always working to our timescale).

That's before we get to our biggest obstacle to effective time management: the appearance, or more likely the non-appearance, of the big idea—the Eureka moment. In Chapter 9 we'll look at how ideas are generated and how creativity can be boosted, but for the moment we'll note that waiting—and searching—for the big revelation is one of the main reasons why designers find it difficult to manage their time. Good ideas are not like Swiss trains; no amount of timetabling and careful scheduling guarantees the arrival of a good idea.

Of course, there are smart, disciplined designers who manage their time with metronomic precision; they stick to internal deadlines; they coordinate their activities with others, and deliver when they say they will. While we might admire these Titans of Personal Time Management, there is no direct link between the ability to manage time and the quality of work produced. There is, however, a link between professionalism and time management—the surest way to lose a client is to miss a deadline. It is for this reason, as well as for our personal sanity, that we have to learn how to handle time.

The greatest impediment to managing time is not time itself, it's anxiety—that sense of sweaty fear that builds up as deadlines loom and time slips away like water through our fingers. Before we go any further, it's worth noting that a sliver of nervy tension is probably necessary when faced with a deadline; if we have no anxiety, it's most likely a sign that we're lacking in passion and commitment. Yet too much flooding of the neural pathways with toxic anxiety is harmful to the creative process.

For me, the breakthrough in time management came when I had a minor revelation about the nature of time. It was hardly a revelation to make Professor Hawking think he had a rival in cosmological insights, but it opened a tiny door that enabled me to cope better with time-based anxiety. Think about waiting an hour for a train in a lonely, threatening railroad station late at night. It will be the longest hour of your life. Now imagine an hour spent watching a favorite movie or TV show—the sixty minutes will pass so fast you'll swear it was only thirty minutes. Yet an hour is an hour, so what's the difference between the hour in the train station and the hour in front of a screen? The only difference is our perception of that hour: we determine whether it is slow or fast.

The realization that it was me, and not my client or my collaborators, or even the clock, who controlled the rate at which time passed, taught me to be less anxious about time. I still feel the pinprick of anxiety when faced with deadlines, but I counter it by remembering that time is in my control. One of the ways I do this is by chopping projects into manageable chunks and breaking each job into a series of small milestones. By reducing time to a number of achievable goals—rather than one big remote horizon—our control is far greater.

An even more important aspect of time management is determining the order in which we do things. Every project has a part—or parts—that we don't like. We'll call them *the late-night railroad station* parts. Yet instead of dealing with these tasks first, most of us make the error of leaving them till last. Big mistake. This warps our sense of time and our ability to manage our energies. Wherever possible, we should do the opposite and tackle the nasty parts first.[2]

Here is a perfect example of doing what I advise against. This chapter and Chapter 8 are both new. All the others are rewrites of existing chapters. Writing fresh chapters is much harder work than adapting existing ones. So what did I do? I wrote them last. Beware of people who tell you what to do but don't practice [2] what they preach.

**How to be a graphic designer, without losing your soul**

Here's another fundamental law of time planning. During the life of most projects, we have highs and lows. This is inevitable. Essential, even (see Chapter 9 [Creative Process]). But we should always avoid ending any interim stage of a project on a low note. When struggling with a task we are often tempted to abandon it, telling ourselves that we'll attack the problem tomorrow with renewed vigor. This occasionally works. It clears the mind and allows us to start afresh. But more usually it means that we restart the project with a lack of enthusiasm, and find distractions and reasons for doing other things. If, on the other hand, we abandon a project on a high note, then we find that we are keen to get back to work—which means that we don't waste time prevaricating.

This brings us to yet another golden rule of time management: when we plan our time, we usually imagine uninterrupted time, or time filled exclusively with our project. In reality, this rarely happens. It is inevitable that interruptions, disruptions, and disasters will happen—clients turn up unexpectedly; the job we finished and sent off three days ago comes back in need of urgent amendments; the train that was supposed to get us to work early breaks down and we arrive late. We should therefore build allowances for setbacks into our thinking and planning. It will make deadlines slightly easier to deal with, and help reduce the readings on our internal "anxiety-o-meters."

3  *Design Dictionary:*  Sir Christopher
   *Perspectives on*  Frayling, British
   *Design Terminology,*  educationalist
   Birkhäuser, 2008.  4  and writer.

## Research

There is an entry on research in the *Design Dictionary*.[3] The author of the article notes that the writer and educator Christopher Frayling[4] identifies three types of design research: research into, for, and through design.

In my frequent visits to design schools, I've noticed a huge interest among students in this latter activity: *research through design*. This fusing of research and design is clearly attractive to a new generation of designers who have grown up with—and been educated in—a definition of graphic design that goes beyond designing shampoo labels. But for the purposes of this chapter, I am mainly interested in research *for* design.

The *Design Dictionary* defines research for design as supporting "in specific ways the (practical, active) process of design whose product is an artifact…." In other words, it's research that leads to a design outcome. This sort of research is often identified as "problem-solving." I've never been attracted to the idea of designers solely as problem-solvers. Designers are often good at solving problems, but by defining design purely as the finding of solutions to problems it is implied that it is only of use when there is a problem in the first place. However, designers are capable of much more. They're capable of imagining the unimaginable, and offering insights and innovations that come from intuition and the rebel yell of creativity (see p.101 [Design Thinking]).

I've often been handed a small forest of paper by a client and told "here's the research we've commissioned. Read it and then get back to us with your creative proposal." Sometimes this "research" is useful, but it's not really research; mostly it's background information—raw data —received from focus groups and the responses to market research questionnaires. Clients like it because it helps them to make pragmatic business decisions and reduce risk. But it can be dangerous for designers because it usually only tells us what has happened in the past. It acts as a straitjacket for creative thinking rather than a springboard for creative interpretation.

There's another sort of research clients like: data mining. This is defined as studying recorded information to detect patterns of behavior. Businesspeople are good at seeing these patterns, but designers can sometimes see something else: opportunities and ways of creating the new and the different. Designers can take this information and translate it into *difference*.

I'm not saying that designers don't need to do research or that they should rely solely on intuition. What I am saying, however, is that designers need to weld research (reading, visiting, touching, tasting) to creative intuition. Research and creativity should go hand in hand.

In 2007, I interviewed the head of branding group Wolff Olins for the British magazine *Creative Review*.[5] It was shortly after the furor caused by the company's design of the logo for the London 2012 Olympic Games. Wolff Olins is a major player in international branding. The group employs designers, business experts, and researchers. I asked CEO Brian Boylan about the company's process. Was it research-driven? "Our process is about getting a deep understanding of our clients," he said, "which is why we have people who come from a more strategic and business background. But then we start exploring, and that's where the intuition comes in. All in all, from beginning to end, it's a creative process, as opposed to a step-by-step logical process. Because if you only followed a logical process you'd inevitably arrive at a dry answer. Some of the answers we arrive at are beyond logical processes."

5   creativereview.co.uk/
    cr-blog/2008/january/
    wolff-olins-expectations-
    confounded

This was music to my ears: when design becomes totally research-driven it becomes logical, but it also becomes reactive rather than visionary. It becomes sterile rather than imaginative. Here's an example of what I'm talking about.

I was once asked to launch, design, and edit a house journal for a membership organization that was widely regarded as being out of touch and off the radar—a view confirmed by the heads of the organization that hired me. The body already had a magazine that was seen as outdated in both content and design, and too narrow in its editorial focus. I was told that the new magazine was required to spearhead change. Somewhat controversially, they also wanted a publication that would work for its membership *and* compete commercially on newsstands. It was a tall order, so I started by talking to both members and non-members.

**How to be a graphic designer, without losing your soul**

I love talking to people who I'm producing design for. It's rarely an option, but when the opportunity presents itself it makes a huge difference to the outcome. Talking to members, it became clear that there was not much appetite for change. They wanted the status quo to be maintained and had no interest in a new magazine that appealed to a non-membership audience.

What was I to do? Here was "research" that was pointing me in the opposite direction of my brief—and my instincts. If I followed the research, I'd end up with a magazine that was like the existing version, and one that would have no chance of success on the newsstands.

I spent hours in magazine stores looking at the state of magazine design. The publication was for the creative sector, but I deliberately avoided looking at this area; instead I looked at magazines in non-related sectors. I also looked at how other entities—companies, products, services—reinvented themselves. I asked questions. I made calculations. And then I made a creative leap. I appointed a radical design company to give the magazine a sharp, unpredictable look, and I adopted a radical editorial tone.

After the first edition appeared, I went onto an online forum to discuss the magazine with the organization's members. The new publication was widely dismissed as too radical and divorced from its traditional roots. It was called "irrelevant," and a "step too far." I felt defeated and wrong-footed. But then something else happened. The magazine started selling in stores; it won design awards; the organization received press coverage that they'd not previously had; and most intriguingly of all, some of the old-guard members started to view the magazine more favorably.

The organization's leaders were happy because their image improved; the magazine became a flagship for the body's new growth. It's true that some of the more traditional members were left behind. I didn't feel any pride in this, but it is impossible to please everyone (something clients often fail to accept), and I knew there had to be casualties. In the end, even the detractors become less voluble.

So what sort of research should we do *for* design? Well, we might begin with a review of what—if anything—has gone before. Finally, we might grill our clients. No matter how focused our idea is on the end user, we have another audience—our clients—the gatekeepers. We always have to get our ideas past them, and we do this best by questioning them, and even contradicting them where necessary.

Design in its purest sense is research mixed with imagination. Both are useful, but best when combined, and next to useless when divorced from each other.

## Strategy

In the eyes of many clients, the strategy that supports design is more important than the design itself. Hardly surprising, since clients don't think like designers—they think like strategists. If we want to communicate with our clients we have to think like strategists, too.

Yet there's a danger here: when all the emphasis is on strategic and tactical thinking, there's a tendency for ideas, intuition, and imagination to be downgraded and pushed to the end of the food chain, with the result that most design that is strategically driven is often characterized by sameness and timidity. It's as if all the thinking gets done at the strategic stage and then the poor designer is left to try to produce a creative response from a suffocatingly narrow list of possibilities. It's as if someone asks a tailor to make them a suit. The tailor makes the suit using all the latest information on fabrics, body-shape statistics, and fashion trends, but forgets to actually measure up the person who ordered the suit.

When design is made to fit strategy rather than developed simultaneously, the result is an ill-fitting suit. Conversely, when design is produced without any strategic underpinning, it is less likely to be accepted by hard-nosed clients. The simple fact is that in the commercial realm we have to combine our designer's intuition with business pragmatism. To put it another way, creativity has to be melded with strategy.

I mentioned Wolff Olins above. Of all the big design and branding groups, they seem to have succeeded in the seamless integration of strategic business thinking with intuitive creativity: "The fundamental thing, though," claims CEO Brian Boylan, "is that it's not all done sequentially. It's not about arriving at a strategy, full stop, and then handing it over to other people and saying now illustrate this strategy."

Of course, not all clients require design to be strategically based: some trust designers to know what will function without the need for it to be strategized to death. But these clients are becoming rare. As businesses and institutions of all kinds—commercial, charitable, cultural, social—become more systematic and more averse to risk, the need to hardwire every design decision with strategy grows more pressing.

So what is the role of strategy in design? It means combining research with market or audience intelligence; it means combining knowledge of technological developments with current patterns of behavior; it means evaluating expenditure in relation to effectiveness; and it means having a grasp of human psychology and behavior and familiarity with trends, fashions, and customs.

Take the example of being asked to design a web site to warn young people against the dangers of illegal drugs. Instinct—or perhaps our clients—might tell us that a lurid visual approach with gothic type and funereal imagery is the correct approach. But in order to formulate an effective strategy we need to talk to people involved in the project and the target audience (research); we need to look at how the target group uses the Internet and other forms of media (analysis); we need to question conventional wisdom (interrogation); and finally we need to use creative intuition (creativity). When this cocktail is shaken, we can arrive at conclusions that will have tactical purpose.

Sometimes, of course, we don't have access to our intended audience, or data that can be analyzed. Sometimes an idea arrives that we know is the right idea but we are flummoxed as to *why* it's the right idea. When this happens we need to indulge in a bit of sleight of hand—or, to put it more grandly—we need to post-rationalize.

Designers often joke about post-rationalizing their work. It is seen as "cheating" or at least a cause for mild embarrassment. But I don't think there's necessarily anything wrong with it. The unconscious mind plays a part in the creative process—we don't always know where ideas come from or why they appear, yet we know they are right. And since there are few clients who find this sort of "unsupported" creativity acceptable, we have to find ways of explaining it to them. After all, if it stands up to scrutiny, how wrong can it be?

**How to be a graphic designer, without losing your soul**

Presentation skills

No matter what stage we are at in our careers, we have to be able to present our ideas to others. If we can't talk about our work with objectivity and if we can't put ourselves into the shoes of the people we are presenting to, we will find life as a graphic designer difficult and dispiriting. No client in the history of the world ever accepted an idea—regardless of how dazzlingly brilliant—without subjecting it to scrutiny and asking questions ("why have you chosen blue?"). If we can't answer questions like this, we run the risk of having a drawer full of brilliant ideas marked "Rejected." In fact, presentation is the most fundamental aspect of what it means to be a designer, and many ideas get rejected not because they are bad ideas but because they are badly presented.

The ability to present work doesn't just mean the ability to present to a boardroom of hard-nosed business people. When a student shows work to a tutor—that's a presentation. When a junior designer shows work to a creative director—that's also a presentation. And when we show an idea to a supplier, collaborator, or colleague—that too is a presentation. Of course, there are formal presentations and there are informal presentations—but they are all presentations, and the better we are at doing them, the more likely we are to have our ideas understood and accepted.

In Chapter 7, which is devoted to clients, I go into the procedural aspects of making a design presentation. At this stage, I only want to stress the importance of presentation as an essential professional skill, and to stress the need to make presentations from the heart and not a manual. By this, I mean it is fine to be yourself. I've dipped into manuals on presentation and they merely add to the stress of presenting. At my old studio we even looked into the value of going on a presentation course, but in the end decided against it. The reason we decided this was because design, in our view, was about conviction and no amount of formal presentation techniques would improve our conviction. I know many excellent designers who are not technically good at presenting, but they talk about their work with such obvious fervor that it doesn't matter. Anything that stems the flow of conviction is bad, in my view.

But as you will see in Chapter 7, there are simple steps we can take to make our presentations more effective: how and when we physically show our work; what we say and when we say it; and how we allow our clients time to think and respond. These are simple procedural techniques that are fundamental to the success or failure of a presentation. They can be learned—or adapted—as each designer sees fit. What cannot be learned, however, is conviction. That has to be grown internally.

Writing skills

I learned to write by composing design proposals. During the 1990s, as design became more competitive, more sophisticated, and more client-driven, I noticed that every major project required a written submission of some sort—even if it was only the letter of introduction to a prospective client or a written statement of our studio credentials.

Sometimes written proposals comprised the entire creative proposal—no images, just words. It was also the case that many clients were more comfortable with a written proposal than a visual one.

I quickly noticed that if I wanted my written submissions to be read, I would have to learn to write with precision, brevity, and the total eradication of waffle. So I learned to write in short, sharp sentences, and I discovered that the most important aspect of writing is what gets left out. The writer's best tool is the delete key. It is rare to find a block of text or sentence that can't be improved by deletions.

Today, it is normal for clients to demand written proposals for even the smallest jobs. I never mind doing this. It helps clarify my thinking—and if a creative proposal can't be expressed in a few words, it is probably wrong. Written proposals are also a way of avoiding doing speculative creative work that gives away our most valuable asset—visual creativity—although many designers argue, correctly in my view, that written proposals are creative acts and should not be given away free either (see p. 24 [Pitching]).

It's clear that writing is a useful skill for any designer. Yet apart from a final-year dissertation or research paper, graphic designers are not encouraged to write at design school. This is odd, since words are the designer's raw materials, much as coal is the raw material of the coal miner. Designers often say they can't write. This is also odd, since many designers have a verbal facility for sharp phrases and economical expression. Most designers are better with words than they realize.

This shyness with written language is partly caused by designers believing that they need to do everything visually. There's a fear that they are betraying their design skills if they exhibit language skills. Yet the ability to handle text is a priceless attribute. Just think how often we struggle to make coherent typographic statements when forced to work with clumsy language: think of all those tortuous line breaks and bad configurations of type that could be eliminated with a few text edits. The ability to suggest and make text changes can often rescue work from second-rate status.

We can only do this if we are confident with language—and, of course, if we have the trust of our clients. Look at many of the great designers who have achieved lasting eminence— Paul Rand, Jan Tschichold, Otl Aicher. They all had language skills and weren't afraid to show them. It's equally true of contemporary designers such as Michael Bierut, Jeffery Keedy, and Ellen Lupton.

However, designers writing about design and designers reading about design is no longer something that happens only in design schools. This change can be partly explained by the huge rise in the number of design books published over the past two decades. Yet perhaps an even bigger impetus has come from the plethora of design blogs that have filled cyberspace in recent years. The visitor figures for these blogs are phenomenal; far more than any print magazine could hope to achieve.

The rise in blogging doesn't necessarily mean that design has been flooded with a new verbal fluency. Most blogs are self-congratulatory and self-promoting. But many are not. Many are serious attempts to promote a discourse around design. This has not been seen before in design and it is a cause for optimism in the ability of designers to express themselves in written form.

**How to be a graphic designer, without losing your soul**

But what if we are not comfortable using written language? For many skilled designers, producing texts takes them to a territory where they feel stretched and exposed. Here are three things I do to create credible texts:

1      After completing a piece of writing, I change the font, column measure, and point size, and then re-read everything. This simple procedure breaks down reading patterns and throws up oddities that were previously invisible or glided over. Like pinning visual work up on the wall, it gives us distance and a fresh perspective, and never fails to show up problems and deficiencies.

2      Rewrite, rewrite, rewrite. How the great writers of the past worked in pen and ink is a mystery to me. Writing without the cut-and-paste function is unthinkable. My first drafts are always garbage, but by the sixth or seventh version I'm beginning to make sense. Also, I've learned to never be satisfied with any sentence, paragraph, or article I've written.

3      Finally, I always try to allow as much time as possible to elapse between completing the final version and committing it to print. Just as changing the font allows us to see mistakes and problems, it is essential to allow time to pass before declaring a text finished. The longer the gap between finishing and reviewing, the better. I've never read anything I've written and not wanted to change something.

I've just remembered—there's a fourth rule. Almost without exception, all great writers have an editor—someone who goes through the text and picks out flaws, mistakes, misjudgements, and criminal libels. Personally, I love the editing process. Anything I've written has only ever been improved as a result of good editing. Of course, it's impractical to expect to have the services of a good editor when we are writing a proposal, a letter of introduction, or our credentials. But we can do the next best thing and ask a friend, colleague, or anyone with an objective view to read our text and highlight anything that doesn't make sense. They will always find something.

Okay, this really is the last rule: always write in plain English and avoid jargon. Even if your client uses business-speak and peppers his or her speech with acronyms and gobbledygook, it doesn't mean you have to.

# How to be a graphic designer, without losing your soul

This chapter can be skipped by designers who have been working for a few years or by anyone with an excess of confidence and self-belief. It is intended for people who have recently graduated, for those who are in the first few years of their careers and have yet to find the job that suits them best, and for designers who suffer occasional bouts of self-doubt and loss of confidence. In other words: normal designers.

Normal people need a job to earn money for shelter, food, books, music, and other life-sustaining essentials. But for designers there is a far more important consideration: we need to start learning how to be a graphic designer. The one thing they never tell us in design school prospectuses is that the real reason we go to design school is to learn how to learn. This is because, after four or five years of hard study,[1] we all need to go back to the beginning and start again. In my experience, a graduate fresh from design school takes between six and eighteen months to become an effective and contributing member of a studio—and that is with careful shepherding and plenty of attention. There are, occasionally, design graduates who emerge from full-time education as thoroughly rounded individuals ready to deal with professional life. But they are rare, and most graduates need to go back to the starting line.

How do you find that first job, and how do you know which job is right for you? The first thing to remember is that in our early career there are very few wrong jobs. Even in the scummy places where designers are treated abysmally, there are lessons to be learned and career firsts to be notched up. This is not the same as saying you must accept the first job that comes along. We all need experience and we need to be working, and everything we see and touch makes us better designers.

Few tasks tax the fledgling designer more than finding a first job. It is an unfairly severe test to have to face at a time when we are least equipped to deal with it.[2] Some people do it effortlessly; others take years to find their niche; a few never find theirs. But over the next few pages, I will provide pointers to help make the process of job-hunting less painful.

Before we begin, I should mention that the two best designers I ever employed broke every rule I am about to give you: neither conducted themselves in their job interviews in a way that I would recommend, and neither had portfolios that inspired immediate confidence. Yet both had unmistakable qualities that shone through their lack of interview savvy, and both exhibited a diamond-hard conviction that disarmed me and, against my rational judgement, convinced me to employ them.

[1] As the design writer Steven Heller noted in an article titled "What this country needs is a good five-year Design Program" on the AIGA website (www.journal. aiga.org): "Proficiency in requisite technologies, not to mention a slew of optional techniques, easily takes a year or more to master in a rudimentary way. Acquiring fluency in the design language(s), most notably type, is an ongoing process. Then there is instruction and practice in a variety of old and new media—print and web, editorial and advertising, static and motion, not to mention drawing and photography—these take time to learn, no less to hone. And what about the liberal arts: writing, history, and criticism?

"Theory is also a useful foundation if taught correctly, but it is often perfunctorily shoehorned into studio classes. How can a design student function without verbal expertise, let alone the ability to read and research? This must also be taught in an efficient manner that takes time. And then there is basic business acumen; every designer must understand fundamental business procedures, which are virtually ignored in the ultimate pursuit of the marketable portfolio."

[2] The designer and blogger Armin Vit writes: "Being a young graphic designer is not easy, physically or emotionally. We enter the field with talent, potential, and personality as our primary assets at an age (average of 23) where we are not exactly kids anymore but surely not responsible adults yet." "The Young and Not So Restless," *Voice: AIGA Journal of Design*, June 4, 2004.

To make matters worse, both took an age to become effective studio members, although ultimately they each turned out to be brilliant designers. My point here is that I believe there is nearly always a valid alternative way of doing everything, and if by doing things your own way and following your own instincts you choose to travel down a different path, then go ahead. In a world of conformity, "different" is good.

In this chapter we'll look at finding a job in an in-house studio within a corporation or institution, and at landing a job in an independent design studio. We'll weigh up the pros and cons of each, and we'll discuss ways to approach both options.

## Working in-house

Sometimes when it comes to finding a job, the correct path is already chosen for us. If you want to be a magazine designer, for example, you will almost certainly have to take a job in a publishing house, since most magazines are designed in-house—although there are some independent design studios that produce magazines for publishing-sector clients. The same might apply to packaging designers; many retailers and manufacturers run in-house studios to produce their own packaging. Similarly, many businesses employ in-house web designers; broadcasters and television stations often have teams of moving-image designers; museums, galleries, and cultural organizations typically employ in-house teams.

"Working in-house" is often dismissed as an inferior option to working in an independent studio, but it can be equally rewarding. Working in-house means that we often get a chance to learn about the world of business, we familiarize ourselves with the conventions of the workplace, and we gain an education that will stand us in good stead in later life if we set up our own studio. We might also earn more money than if we work in an independent design studio, and we might enjoy a period of financial security at a time when we need to be devoting all our energies to learning our craft and not being distracted by the problems that can afflict small design studios (bad debts, the slog of finding new work, punishing deadlines).

*Design Week* ran an article investigating the pros and cons of working in-house in the UK. It listed the benefits as: "More civilized working hours … better work/life balance." It listed the disadvantages as: "Often located away from the urban design hubs…can have stigma attached."[3] The English designer Chris Ashworth has worked on both sides of the fence. After graduating, he set up his own studio. Subsequently, he worked for an independent design studio and MTV, before succeeding David Carson as art director of *Ray Gun* magazine. He then became creative director of Getty Images, the giant image library. Ashworth views both experiences as differing sharply. He compares independent studio life with working in-house by way of a series of contrasting adjectives: "Instability/stability; isolation/interaction; freedom/collaboration; local/global; notes/briefs."

3   Hannah Booth,
    "Good Company,"
    *Design Week*,
    September 23, 2004.

**How to be a graphic designer, without losing your soul**

The argument most frequently given against working in-house is that the designer is required to work on the same narrow range of projects. This can often be true, but it is not always the case. Besides, in the early stages of a career, there's not much harm in working doggedly at the same task over and over again. Working in-house may sometimes lack the fizz and glamour of life in an independent studio, where working without a metaphorical safety net can be stimulating, but as a first step in a career it is rarely a wrong move.

It is only by meeting people in both environments that we gain sufficient insight to allow us to decide which is best for us. In fact, here's another little nostrum to add to the list that we're accumulating: there's no such thing as a bad interview. Even the bad ones are good; I learned a lot about design and life from being interviewed by people. At the very least it taught me how to treat interview candidates when, years later, I had to interview designers myself. It also taught me how each employer looks for something different, and how important human relationships are in the process of finding a job. It's for these reasons that I recommend attending as many interviews as possible—even unpromising ones (you can always say no if offered a job)—to weigh up the pluses and minuses of life in-house against life in the independent sector, as well as to acquire valuable interview skills.

Working for an independent design studio

Design studios are a mixture of slave camp and enchanted playground; we can always spot the good ones because they maintain a balance between these two polarities. The slave camp resemblance is unavoidable—long hours with not much pay and little recognition. But when we are starting out, we don't mind this because among all the relentless pressure we glimpse moments of enchantment. We see the pleasure that comes from doing good work and making a contribution (singly or collaboratively) to the studio's output. And there's the camaraderie of being with like-minded people. Studio life is often as good as working life gets.[4]

There are, naturally, disappointments, personal rebuffs, and collective failures to be found in studio life. But always remember, there are millions of people who'd swap jobs with us if they could. Stop anyone in the street and ask them what sort of work they'd like to do, and most will reply: "something creative." In our post-industrial world, no one wants to do unrewarding work. We all want the buzz of "making a contribution." Designers are privileged: we get to make something, and we get paid for having smart ideas that affect the lives of, perhaps, millions of our fellow citizens. Remembering this makes the knockbacks easier to take, and it makes it easier to live with the fact that we'll always earn less than merchant bankers.

4   In his profile of Bruce Mau in *Fast Company* (October 2000), Scott Kirsner creates a beguiling snapshot of studio life: "Inside the high-ceilinged loft space on the edge of Toronto's Chinatown are tall metal bookshelves, drafting tables, digital-video editing suites, architectural models, and scores of hard-working professionals. The deadline pressure is palpable, and couriers make breathless entrances and exits throughout the afternoon. Even as 6 p.m. approaches, not one employee makes a move to head for home. Instead, everyone on staff clusters around a tray of fresh fruit brought in by Cathy Jonasson, the firm's vice president and managing director."

### Apprenticeships

It's an unfashionable word with connotations of servility and poverty. We don't tend to have apprenticeships in design; we have work placements, work experience, and internships. But no matter what you call it, we all have to serve an apprenticeship; it is a necessary and unavoidable step on the road to becoming a mature designer. It needn't be a dispiriting experience either. The energizing charge that comes from learning from more experienced designers is invigorating. In design school, everyone is pretty much the same age and pretty much engaged in the same struggle to find a voice and a foothold on the design career path; furthermore, everyone is working, mostly, in the hypothetical realm. But when we start work, the hypothetical becomes the actual; we are suddenly working alongside people who may be well advanced along their career path, and who may be sophisticated and articulate designers who have found their own voice. This can be intimidating. Some young designers never get over the shock of working next to experienced designers and retreat into self-doubt and feelings of inadequacy. It's a decisive moment in a designer's education, and how we deal with it shapes our future. Happily, most find contact with experienced designers inspirational, and it provides a timely impetus for personal development.

Working alongside an experienced designer will teach us more than almost anything else, especially if the designer is generous and helpful—and most designers are generous and helpful. This is the moment when we realize that there are huge gaps in our knowledge; that we don't know how to organize our work; that our typography is unexpectedly raw and crude; that we are tongue-tied with clients, and briefs seem painfully limiting. It is the moment when we decide that we are really not as good as we thought we were.

Some designers, when they reach this realization, erect a protective shell to try to obscure the fact that they are deficient in certain areas. This is dangerous. It is much better to ask for help. Few designers, even when up against punishing deadlines, will refrain from helping a new designer. But you must ask for help: you are serving an apprenticeship, and you will have to be prepared to make a nuisance of yourself if you want to be heard. You will have to show willingness and boundless enthusiasm, and you will have to show that you want to learn.[5]

### Internships

Increasingly, the only way into full-time employment is through an internship. A successful spell as an intern can often lead to job offers. I've employed many designers this way. The designer given an internship must use this primarily as a learning opportunity, but also as an unrivalled opportunity to impress. Look for ways of making yourself indispensable. If it's a small studio, answer the phone if you hear it ringing, and take an accurate message; offer to get sandwiches at lunchtime for overworked colleagues. Always turn up on time, and don't rush out of the door as soon as the day is over. Design is about commitment: if you want to have a nine-to-five existence, get a job in a government tax office.

[5] Armin Vit writes: "As junior designers—the common launching pad for designers—we are expected to pay our dues by working long hours on thankless work that in our view poses no real professional challenge, while learning the ropes in the shadows of Senior Designers, Creative Directors, and Principals. It has worked for decades… but if we are lucky enough to land a job with a prominent designer we can call it an apprenticeship and look back fondly on the experience." "The Young and Not So Restless," *Voice: AIGA Journal of Design*, June 4, 2004.

**How to be a graphic designer, without losing your soul**

We've already noted that the life of a designer is privileged, but there is a price to be paid for this privilege and that price is unflinching commitment. You have to be prepared to make sacrifices.

Not all internships are equally beneficial. A young designer is unlikely to derive any benefits from a studio that offers unpaid internships; it's a sure sign of a studio with low regard for its staff. The same goes for studios that fail to offer tuition, guidance, and on-the-job experience; chances are they are only looking for cheap labor and should be avoided. Just as there is a responsibility on interns to "make sacrifices," there is an equal responsibility on behalf of studios not to exploit interns. I've already noted that all experience is good experience, but no one should be exploited. Last time I looked, slavery had been abolished in most parts of the world; one or two studio bosses need to be reminded of this.

### Finding out about employment opportunities

Before you can land a job, you need to know where to look for jobs. A lucky few get picked on the strength of their degree show, or by impressing a designer visiting the student's school. But for most, it's a matter of looking for vacancies. There are a number of ways of finding out who is hiring. Look in the design press, trawl the Internet, and ask around. You might also consider signing up with a recruitment agency that finds personnel for studios.[6]

Many hirings are made by studio heads ringing acquaintances and asking them if they've seen any hot talent. I've been asked this question many times by friends looking for designers. It means that it's never a waste of time showing your portfolio to anyone who will look at it—you may not get a job offer, but your interviewer might get a call from someone asking if they've seen anyone good.[7]

The most likely route to finding a job is by contacting studios. Start by drawing up a list of your favorites, but remember that your favorites are probably everyone else's favorites, too, so be wary of approaching only the cool, hip studios, or the better-known ones. They get lots of applications from good people, so box clever and look into the less well-illuminated corners of the design world.

[6] Some recruitment agencies are said to be good. My philosophy as an employer of design talent has always been to find talent by my own efforts. The act of looking (attending degree shows, visiting colleges) is a rewarding and informative exercise in itself. Furthermore, I've always believed that there is something lacking in a design company that can't attract a steady flow of talent to its doorstep.

[7] An hour or so after writing these words I was called by a designer friend and asked if I'd seen anyone good recently. You see, it happens all the time!

### Approaching a design studio

When approaching a studio, it is worth remembering that designers are judged on the quality of their approach as much as on the quality of their work. Your phone call, your e-mail, your letter will be scrutinized like a sniffer dog checks for contraband at an airline baggage carousel; get it right and you're halfway there, get it wrong and you could be in for a long hunt for a job.

You'd be amazed how many people make a hash of their initial approach. I've received handwritten letters on ruled paper ripped from spiral-bound notebooks. I've received letters from designers who haven't bothered to design their own letterhead. I've received letters in which the writer couldn't even be bothered to spell my name correctly.[a] Most heinous of all, I've received letters that began "Dear Sir or Madam." I bin anything that begins "Dear Sir or Madam." It tells me everything I need to know about the individual who wrote the letter: if they apply the same lazy, half-cocked approach to their work, trouble will follow just as surely as a black eye follows a punch on the nose.

It's easy to get this stuff right. You decide what approach you want to use—a letter, phone call, or e-mail —and you do it properly. Think of it as your first professional brief: to communicate your unique qualities and capabilities. Not many designers are taught how to do this in design school, so you will have to learn to do it yourself. But it's not difficult.

I favor the old-fashioned letter. It is the least intrusive method of approach, and it allows you to meticulously prepare your proposal. Even more importantly, a letter is an elemental form of graphic communication. It is a good test of your abilities to formulate a message. The rules are simple: first, you must have a letterhead. It needn't be foil-blocked with eighteen Pantone colors. A simple black and white DTP document will do—but sweat blood over it to make it visually arresting and professionally functioning. Letterheads are part of the DNA of graphic design. You're not much of a graphic designer unless you've designed a successful letterhead, and the rise of e-mail hasn't made them any less important.

Once you've targeted a studio, you need to find out who is responsible for recruiting. This necessitates research. Web sites will often give you this information, but if not, make a phone call to get the name (and spelling) of the person you need to write to. When you're making the call it's worth remembering that, if the company has a receptionist, this is an important person. Receptionists often double up as administrators and they are usually influential figures with a finely developed sense of who should have access to their employers and co-workers. As a general rule, it is worth being polite to receptionists (it is worth being polite to everyone), but it is doubly so in the case of design company receptionists. They are a powerful breed with good instincts about who will "fit in" and who won't.

Having found the name of the person responsible for recruiting, a good letter is now required. The rules are simple. Make your letter short (one sheet only). Make it literate and to the point. Say who you are, what you do, and what you want. Nothing else. Well, there is one other thing you could add: a line or two of mild flattery. State that you are aware of Studio X's marvelous work for Client Y, and that you have found it inspirational. Don't lay it on too thick, but designers are vain and will respond with Pavlovian slavering to a bit of mild, but honest, praise. It also shows that you know something about the work of the company that you are applying to.

If there are no openings (highly likely), it is easy for an employer to brush you off with "Sorry, no vacancies." For this reason, it is always wise to request an interview, not a job. It is much less easy to refuse a request for an interview, and most designers are kind-hearted, sympathetic characters who have traveled the same path as you, and will, with a bit of friendly cajoling, agree to a portfolio review. Exploit the innate kindness of designers.

[a] This is not vanity. My name is not easy to spell. But if an applicant can't be bothered to get it right, it suggests they might be slap-dash or lazy in other matters of detail— an unacceptable failing in a graphic designer.

**How to be a graphic designer, without losing your soul**

Next, you need to include some samples of work. If you are a moving-image designer, a web designer, or a multimedia designer you might feel the need to send a disk. Try to resist this urge. Instead, add a few sheets of Letter-sized (A4) paper showing stills or frames from your work laid out in a clear and precise manner. Designers in busy studios (and you should assume that they are all busy—if they are not, they definitely won't be hiring) rarely have time to stop and look at disks and tapes; it is too time-consuming. It is much better to give them something to provoke an instant response and prompt them to offer to see you. If they agree to see you, then you can show disks or tapes. Sending an e-mail with a link to a web site is acceptable.

If you are job-hunting in a period when design is in the economic doldrums (roughly every ten years, in my experience), you might have to write so many letters and attend so many fruitless interviews that you begin to wonder about the wisdom of becoming a designer. But persistence, doggedness, and barefaced cheek will pay off.[9]

9   I don't, however, recommend that you turn up unannounced at studios. Although I once had a young designer turn up and demand that I interview him: I was impressed with his chutzpah, so I agreed. I ended up offering him a job on the spot—but he was a sort of genius.

The worst thing that can happen is that you become disheartened. If your search for a job is going badly, you must urgently reassess. You must search for ways of refining your presentation. Try rewriting your letter and changing the work samples you're sending. If they are not getting a response, perhaps they're not as sharp or as effective as you think they are. You might also be targeting the wrong people, so rethink your list of potential employers. Reassessment and rigorous self-appraisal are the keys to being a good designer.

It's also worth considering doing things that attract attention and bring potential employers to you. In the 1960s, the wonderful Italian designer, the late Germano Facetti, decorated the ceiling of a friend's bookstore in London. It was seen by the founder of Penguin Books, Allen Lane, who appointed Facetti to restyle the Penguin imprint—for which he has become justly famous. You might, however, choose to avoid the ruse used by the designer who sent a box of live locusts to the creative director of a well-known British advertising agency, in an attempt to get noticed. The creative director invited the young hopeful to an interview, where he revealed himself to be an ardent animal-lover and proceeded to berate the unfortunate interviewee for his cruelty to living creatures.

The interview

If you get your approach right, you will be invited to interview. Look at each interview as a substantial victory. Think about what you've achieved by getting an interview: you've persuaded a busy creative director, senior designer, or studio head to stop what they are doing and give you their time and attention. Congratulations. You should be pleased.

In interviews, your character is under as much scrutiny as your work. How you conduct yourself is as important as the work you show. You can begin by being on time, and being friendly and considerate. If this sounds obvious to you, I apologize, but I've come across many candidates who don't think these details are the least bit important. Don't assume, either, that you have unlimited time. Your interviewer may specify a time limit, but make sure your presentation can be delivered in under fifteen minutes (this includes small talk and admiring comments about the studio's tasteful web site and the brochure that you picked up in reception).

I am now going to say something so obvious you will be tempted to stop reading this book and throw it away. Don't. Even if this is a crime you are not guilty of, pass the information on to others, because there are many offenders; I should know, I've interviewed dozens of designers who've committed this monstrous offense. What am I talking about? Spitting at the interviewer? Calling into doubt the interviewer's personal hygiene? No, worse. I'm talking about designers who show their portfolios to themselves. I used to keep quiet about this. When a designer sat down in front of me and showed me half of their portfolio, while they viewed the other half, I'd remain silent and crane my neck. Now I say, in my best schoolteacher voice: "Excuse me, who are you showing your portfolio to?" This is usually met with bewilderment, and it's only when I grab the portfolio and turn it to face me, that the realization of what they are doing sinks in. So here's the rule: when showing a portfolio, turn it to face the interviewer. If your work is on a laptop, then do the same with the laptop—position the screen directly in front of the interviewer (it is perfectly acceptable to plonk yourself next to your interviewer so that you can operate the machine). I told you it was simple, but you'd be astonished by how many designers don't bother to turn their work to face the person, or persons, they are showing it to.10 Interviewing someone who does this is a bit like going to a gig and having a pillar in front of you. The first law of presentation is: let your interviewer see the work.

Talk succinctly about your work. Avoid excessive detail and allow the interviewer to ask questions. An interviewer who doesn't ask questions is probably not interested in your work. Be alert to the microclimate of the interview; signs of inattentiveness and distraction in the interviewer mean that you are not getting through. Either your work, or your personality, is not captivating him or her, so you must alter your approach. The most likely cause is that you are giving too much information. Your interviewer will be capable of assessing your work without long rambling descriptions, so only give enough information to support what the viewer can see for him or herself. Go through it quickly, but don't rush it, and allow the interviewer to dictate the pace. Be passionate and proud of your work, show that you care deeply about what you do, but also show that you are not complacent and that you strive for improvement.

Once you have shown your work, wait for the interviewer to comment. If you are lucky, you will get an instant verdict. Even if the verdict is unfavorable, you are being given valuable information, so use it to realign your approach in readiness for the next interview.

If you've made a big splash and your interviewer is interested in you, you might be asked what sort of salary you want. Tread carefully: this question means that the studio has no policy on salaries. Don't be drawn on this. Say that you need enough money to live on, and that you are open to reasonable offers, and leave it at that. Most studios know what they can afford, and are only trying to get you on the cheap.

10 Shortly after writing these words, I gave a talk to some students at one of the larger English design colleges. I mentioned that young designers often "showed their portfolios to themselves." One or two students laughed disbelievingly. Later that day, I did a series of workshops with four or five groups of students. Most of them had been working on a project set by a local radio station. I agreed to offer a critique of the work to date. The first student to show me her efforts laid her work out in front of herself, making it impossible for anyone else to view it. I pointed this out to her and said how pleased I was she'd done it, because I doubted that my audience had believed me earlier when I said that this was a common mistake made by young designers.

**How to be a graphic designer, without losing your soul**

If you are offered a job on the spot—it happens—you should ask for written confirmation (a good studio will do this anyway) and you can now go and celebrate. A more likely scenario is that the interviewer will request that you "keep in touch." This is also a good sign. It shows that you have made a mark, but most importantly it gives you a "contact." In other words, here is someone who you can legitimately approach again in a few months' time. After a dozen good interviews you may not have any job offers, but you will have accumulated a great address book. Everyone you see becomes a contact.

### The follow-up

After every interview you need to leave something behind. Ideally something small, striking, and easily stored. A postcard with contact details pinned to a sheet of Letter-sized (A4) paper showing two or three of your best pieces of work will do. Or you can be adventurous and produce something innovative—a handmade (or printed) booklet, for example. At the end of one interview I conducted with a young designer, I was given a Ledger-sized (A3) poster, covered in a tangle of graphic equations and symbols. It was a complex graph charting his attempts to find work, and listed every designer and studio he'd approached (including some famous names). The poster carried verbatim telephone conversations and reproduced e-mails (including one of my own), few of which showed the senders in a good light. I was impressed with his audacity and graphic diligence, but I also couldn't help being a tiny bit offended by seeing my private e-mail reproduced. He didn't get the job, which is not to say he wasn't good.

The task of promoting yourself to your newly acquired network of contacts is critical. You mustn't be overzealous; you need to be sparing but effective. E-mails or letters are best —although phone calls can also work, since your target knows who you are, and will be less reluctant to talk to you than before. Here you will see the benefits of cultivating relationships with studio receptionists. But don't become a pest. It's a fine line between being a nuisance and keeping prospective employers informed about your activities.

Consider designing some sort of mailer. It should be something striking and confident and show that you have made progress since your previous interview. To achieve this you may need to create some self-initiated projects to keep it stoked with new work. Design letterheads for friends or websites for unsigned bands; do anything to keep your hand in and to expand your portfolio.

### Personal portfolios

Your portfolio is your store window. It doesn't matter whether it is a printed portfolio or a laptop presentation, the same rules apply: make it as compelling and as revealing as possible. Push yourself. Don't think, "oh, this will do." It won't. After your personality, it is the second most valuable tool that you possess to help you find a job.

A portfolio of eight to ten interesting pieces of work is ideal. Any more and you risk dragging out the interview. Avoid duplication; if you have two similar projects, be ruthless and only show one. Ideally your work should be printed out as high-quality inkjet color outputs. The advantages of this are that it is cheap and allows frequent updates. Make sure your printouts are of the highest quality. They should be loose individual sheets, which allow the interviewer to hold them and look at them freely. Loose sheets, covered in replaceable acetate, are preferable to sheets clipped together in a ring binder (attaching them and detaching them can be distracting).11 Each page is a mini-portfolio. It can show the finished job, or it can show developmental work. I wouldn't recommend anything larger than size C (A2). There is something off-putting about a huge portfolio—plus it's a health hazard if you are out on a windy day.

A designer friend of mine recently told me that he wouldn't consider a designer—no matter how talented—for a position in his studio if his or her work 11 was presented in a portfolio with ring-binder clips. "I'd sooner take on someone with a forked tail and horns," he said.

Your portfolio sheets should exhibit a degree of uniformity. Create a grid, and make sure every project adheres to the grid. This might be difficult because you will probably be showing a variety of projects (2D and 3D), but it's worth trying to get this right because you will be judged on how your work is presented as much as by the work itself. A portfolio that has an underlying unity and structure will score more points (and be more enjoyable to view) than one that has no structure or cohesion.

Print designers will naturally want to show finished specimens—printed books, brochures, letterheads. Hand these over to the interviewer immediately, and don't flick through them admiringly as if you were seeing them for the first time—people do, I promise you.

I'd avoid sketchbooks. To seasoned employers, they all tend to look the same. It is like new parents showing you a picture of their baby: enchanting to them, less so to those without biological ties to the adored infant. However, I'm sure there are employers who like to look at sketchbooks; if you have one that you are especially proud of, bring it along, but I suggest that you only show it if asked to. Working drawings are more useful. Some designers place great importance on them. But not every item of work needs to be accompanied by working drawings. Two or three at most will suffice, and only if they show clear developmental thinking.

What sort of physical portfolio should you have? A bag or box that is easy to open, that allows your work to be viewed easily and that protects the work as you scurry from interview to interview. Keep your portfolio clean. It should not look as if it lives in a mildewed cellar when not being used. No employer will expect a custom-made flight-case designed by Philippe Starck, but valuable points can be won for a distinctive case or carrier. Remember, your interviewer has probably had years of looking at identical slim black portfolio bags, so a nicely designed, unostentatious box will strike a refreshing note.

One last thing: mark your portfolio in some way so that when you open it, it is ready for viewing. It can be distracting to see a portfolio opened upside down, and have to wait while it is turned over. It's a tiny detail, but your success might depend on tiny details. We'll talk more about portfolios when we get to the subject of studio portfolios (where the approach is different).

**How to be a graphic designer, without losing your soul**

What do employers really want?

Ask a hundred employers this question and you will get a hundred different answers, but my guess is that they are all looking for someone they get on with. In the intimate and psychologically revealing space of a design studio, we have to "get on" with the people we work with. Keep this in mind when you are being interviewed. Look for ways to reassure a prospective employer that you are hard-working, adaptable, and socially well-adjusted. There is no need to bang on about your talent—an experienced designer will be able to assess your merits as a designer within a few seconds of opening your portfolio. Assessing your personality is harder—the least you can do is help. Stress that you don't mind doing the dreary stuff and that you are happy to assist senior designers; show a willingness to understand the studio's culture; show that you already know something about the studio's work; and most importantly, trust your personality, and trust your work.

Learn to enjoy interviews. View them as precious opportunities to study the thinking and working process of designers and studios; as opportunities to have your work critiqued by your peers; as ways of measuring your progress. Don't be afraid to ask for a blunt assessment of your work, and if the comments seem valid and worthwhile, act on them quickly.

At some time in the future, you will perhaps interview designers yourself, and you will look back on the ordeal of being interviewed with a different perspective. You might also have your early attempts to recruit designers come back to confront you. I was recently introduced to the designer Fred Deakin—a partner in the London-based studio Airside, and a member of the band Lemon Jelly. He told me that I had—many years before—interviewed him. I tensed. I didn't remember the interview (which doesn't say much for my talent-spotting powers). I asked him if the interview had gone well; "Yes," he said. "You were very helpful." I was relieved.

Approaching an in-house studio

All the above applies equally to finding a job within a business that operates an in-house studio, with the possible exception that you might be interviewed by a non-designer; for example, it might be a marketing manager, a communications manager, or the director of the company. Being interviewed by a non-designer requires a slightly different approach. Your interviewer will almost certainly have some knowledge of design, but it might be a rather self-centered interest and stretch no further than his or her own company or products. You will have to compensate for this by using plain language and avoiding design-oriented exposition. You don't have to compromise; you simply have to make allowances for the fact that your interviewer is not a designer.

Conclusion

For a small studio, hiring a graduate—or a junior designer—is not a risk-free undertaking. Try to think about your suitability from the employer's point of view. What are the risks they are assessing? The risk for an employer is mainly financial: even a low salary can put a strain on a studio. There will be other considerations. Will the new individual require lots of attention? Will they fit into the studio culture? Yet the most common concern when assessing a new recruit is calculating how long it will take for this individual to reach effectiveness. The six to eighteen months that I estimate as the time it might take for a graduate to become effective is a perilously long time for a small employer to wait.

Comparison of working as a freelance graphic designer and setting up a studio with others. Or pros and cons of solo life vs. communal life.

**How to be a graphic designer, without losing your soul**

Working as a freelance designer or starting a studio used to be something that was only done by battle-tough designers with decades of experience behind them and at least a few gray hairs. Not so anymore. Today, it is common for graduates and young designers to set up as freelancers—picking up clients wherever they can—or to form studios, collectives, and partnerships. There's no question that a bit of experience helps with either option, but two things are forcing the pace: the first is the huge number of graduates emerging from design schools all over the world; the second is the increasing number of opportunities for designers.

There are pundits and experts who sound alarm bells. They point out that design schools are producing too many graduates, and warn about diminishing rather than increasing opportunities for employment. My strong belief is that they are wrong. Despite the rising numbers of graduates produced by design schools all over the world, opportunities in communication and design-related activities are also rising—they just don't look like the old opportunities. On top of this, the new breed of design graduates is remarkably well equipped to deal with the modern world. Mastery of the basic digital tools, for example, enables anyone to find work, start a business, or engage in Internet-related activities—commercial or cultural.

We may have reached a point where the ability to design and build a simple web site is as important as the ability to drive a car. When I recently interviewed a group of students from one of London's leading design schools, only one of the group wanted a career in conventional commercial graphic design. All the others (about eight or nine people) wanted to work in curating, design management, research, and design-related entrepreneurial activities.

It's worth noting another contemporary phenomenon: the end of the idea of a job for life. In the precarious world of tomorrow, we are all going to have to learn to find work where we can, to change careers if we need to, and to stay permanently flexible. A basic design education and a set of digital skills form a good grounding for this brave new world.

I am under no illusions that there are obstacles and difficulties involved in being freelance or running a studio. There always were. What the advocates of caution fail to understand is that for many graduates and young designers, the life of a designer is about more than a way of earning a living. Design has become extremely popular as a career choice, and with it has come a desire for autonomy, authorship, and, increasingly, the urge to use design for social good. This urge is driving strong-minded designers to take control of their own destinies regardless of the paucity of rewards and regardless of the difficulties.

With all this ringing in our ears, let's take a cold hard look at what it means to be a freelance designer or to start a studio. It's not going to be easy, but nothing worthwhile ever is.

Going freelance

On its web site, under the heading "Occupational Outlook Handbook, 2008–09 Edition," the U.S. Department of Labor notes that in 2006 there were "about 261,000 graphic designers" working in the United States, and that "about 25 percent of them were self-employed." The report goes on to say this about freelance employment: "Because consumer tastes can change quickly, designers also need to be well read, open to new ideas and influences, and quick to react to changing trends. The ability to work independently and under pressure are equally important traits. People in this field need self-discipline to start projects on their own, to budget their time, and to meet deadlines and production schedules. Good business sense and sales ability also are important, especially for those who freelance or run their own firms."[1]

1    bls.gov/oco/ocos090. htm

It's official then: the design world is tough and competitive. So why make it tougher for yourself by setting up as a self-employed freelance designer, with its attendant risks and uncertainties? In my experience, the freelance life suits two types of designers. The first are resourceful individuals with specialist skills—Photoshop wizard, skilled typographer, After Effects specialist, Flash animator. They can charge handsomely for their services, knowing that when their task is finished they are free to move on, or free to have a week at home doing zilch. Initially they may struggle to acquire a sustainable flow of work, but over time these individuals can build up a client base that results in regular commissions.

The second type is best characterized as the creative loner. These are individuals with a strong personal vision that cannot be comfortably accommodated within the structure of a design group or an in-house studio. They are often designers who cannot compromise their work. The Norwegian designer Kim Hiorthøy exemplifies all the best qualities of a freelance, independent-minded designer. He works alone because: "I've always done it and I'm comfortable with it." I asked him in an email conversation to describe the advantages and disadvantages of the freelance life: "I very often change things completely at whim," he states, "and often at the very end of working on something. Not having to explain or argue is an advantage, I think. I know that could sound like a disadvantage as well, but so far it's often felt like it was for the better."

If you get it right—if you are psychologically suited to the life—a freelance existence can be creatively rewarding and financially beneficial. If you have good clients who pay you adequately, and on time, then the monetary benefits from being self-employed are considerable. Financial advisers and tax experts will tell you that it is the most advantageous situation to be in: with careful planning and meticulous administration you can maximize the benefits of being self-employed.

**How to be a graphic designer, without losing your soul**

2   In an interview in *Eye*
    (summer 2000),
    designer Lorraine Wild
    noted the charms of
    garage working:
    "There's something
    very comfortable and
    productive about the
    garage. Being there
    has as much to do
    with adjusting to the
    realities of being a
    parent of a very young
    child as it does to the
    analysis of what is—
    and isn't—necessary
    for the production
    of interesting work. It
    is somewhat of an
    anti-office in that it is
    not about giving one-
    self over entirely to
    maintaining the con-
    temporary corporate
    standard of design
    production. The space
    is configured to the
    work that I want to do.
    Perhaps it has to do
    with my upbringing in
    Detroit, where garages
    are often the site of
    great creativity (both
    automotive and musi-
    cal), or the influence of
    my teacher Paul Rand,
    who worked out of his
    kitchen for years."

You may be able to work from home—in a garage, [2] an attic, or a spare room. But this doesn't suit everyone, and many people find the prospect of being at home all day, every day, unappealing. On a stolidly practical note, working alone means that when you encounter one of those knotty software problems that all designers face, you can't wander over to the next desk and get an instant answer. On your own, you might have to waste hours looking it up in a manual—an activity that can often make us lose the will to live. Yet for others, working from home is highly desirable: no studio rent to pay and no tiring commute every day. You need to think about what your address says about you: will an obviously domestic address make you look cheap and flaky? An increasingly viable alternative to home working is to rent studio space with other like-minded freelance designers. This allows you to retain creative and fiscal control over your life, but at the same time enables you to exchange ideas and share resources.

### Freelance life—pros and cons

You will have to be prepared to do your own finances—tax planning, invoicing, cash-flow control, debt chasing, and banking. In her book *The Professional Practice of Design*, Dorothy Goslett notes: "Many designers, though admitting its necessity, think that design administration is boring, a tiresome chore always to be put aside for doing second if something more exciting crops up to be done first. But good design + good administration = good fees well-earned." Goslett's equation (first written in 1960) may discourage certain individuals, but it is unavoidably true. It is widely assumed that designers are not very good at administration. This is often the case, but by no means universal. Good administration skills can be acquired and become habitual.

Finding work when you are on your own is tough. A printer friend once told me that if you only start looking for work when you need to, then it's too late. What he meant was that you need to be looking for work even when you are busy. Easy to say, and easy to do if you are a big studio with lots of people—but on your own, it becomes a hefty burden. As Goslett notes: "This [finding clients] will be the main battle of your whole freelance career: not only to find clients to start you going but constantly to be finding clients to keep you going. It is a battle which has to be waged more or less ceaselessly until you retire and one which will never allow you to rest on your laurels."

Are you disciplined enough to work on your own? In most studios, there's a healthy sense of communal activity that motivates by contagion—you can't sit about doing nothing when everyone else is working like demons. On your own, it's different. You have to be more disciplined, not less. You have to make your own schedules. You have to resist the allure of the fridge and daytime television (actually, if you can't resist daytime television you should consider a career change). Also, the act of leaving the house every day to go to a place of work, and being out in the world is good for creativity—street posters, architecture, favorite stores, faces in the crowd, galleries, bookstores, going to the sandwich shop at lunchtime—all contribute to the building of an alert design sensibility. Even the ugly stuff —the crass billboards and the trashy magazines on newsstands—informs the way we think about our work. If we remove this from our lives, we risk becoming semi-detached.

You won't need much equipment to get started, but you will need to buy software, furniture, and materials. All this requires a degree of financial planning that you may need help with. You will also need to know how to cost projects and how to charge. These more practical issues are dealt with when we look at how to run a studio. Lastly, there is the perennial problem of late payment. Not many firms worry about making a freelancer wait for his or her money. This puts a strain on cash flow (and nerves), and is the cause of most non-creative problems for the self-employed designer. Spending time chasing up outstanding debts is a vital if unenjoyable activity for the freelance designer.[3]

In the modern business world, aggressive behavior is often thought to be necessary. If a payment is late, you are supposed to yell at someone. My advice is to do the opposite. Approach the individuals concerned with the utmost politeness; make friends with your clients' finance departments—they are rarely the villains. When you get a cheque in the post, call and thank them. Designers like to have their work praised, and so do clerks in accounting offices. [3]

## Who uses freelance designers?

Clients are attracted to freelance designers for the same three reasons that they are attracted to studios or design firms:

1.   Creative reasons – *Does this person do the sort of work I want?*
2.   Personal reasons – *Do I get along with this person?*
3.   Financial reasons – *Will hiring this person be cheaper than hiring a studio?*

In the eyes of many clients, a freelance designer will be a less expensive option than hiring a studio with its bigger overheads. As a freelancer you can use this to your advantage by stressing that you offer all the skills and creativity of a bigger studio but at a lower cost. However, smallness can also work against you; some clients will avoid freelance designers because they prefer the comfort of a studio with a range of dedicated personnel, and are happy to pay the higher fees involved.

**How to be a graphic designer, without losing your soul**

Starting up as a freelance designer requires courage. Without first having a spell in a studio learning the mechanics of running a business, it will prove a steep and intimidating climb. Setting up a freelance practice is, in many ways, no different from starting a company—the only difference is that you are CEO, senior designer, junior designer and office assistant, all in one. As we shall see when we look at starting a studio, one of the great advantages of a company is that you are part of a group. As long as the group has shared goals, there is comfort and strength to be found in the communal nature of a studio. The freelancer, on the other hand, is a solo player and will need reservoirs of personal toughness and self-reliance that group members don't need: just make sure your shoulders are big enough to take the pressure.

## Starting a studio

I've always believed that the buzz to be had from working in an efficient and productive design studio is hard to beat. I'm sure other types of workplace and other sectors can match that claim, but there's something uniquely satisfying about being part of a group of people engaged in the creation of products and outcomes in which the individuals can claim total, shared, or partial authorship. These products and outcomes can be aesthetic, business-focused, or socially centered. It doesn't matter which, just so long as everyone in a studio shares in the ambition, is allowed to contribute to it, and has their contribution recognized.

Authorship—individual and collective—is the key to the success of a design studio. The satisfaction that comes with "authorship" is a fundamental requirement of modern life. Many businesses deny their employees this; they produce rulebooks that dictate behavior and attitude. While this suits some people, it is anathema for others. The good design studio, however, is fueled by the notion that we all want to do meaningful and creative work for which we can claim personal or shared authorship. In the post-industrial world, we want to use our brains, not our muscles; we want to sweat ideas, not bodily fluids. It also helps that studio life is a communal activity, and in the best studios everyone enjoys a sort of equality and a sense of shared endeavor that is rarely encountered elsewhere.

Perhaps all this sounds idealistic? In reality, most design studios are places that are characterized by stress, hard work, and long hours, interspersed with occasional moments of mild euphoria brought on by creative achievement. Put like this, it's hard to imagine why anyone would ever want to set up and run a design studio. Yet the number of designers setting up studios is increasing. The example of Bibliothèque, the designers of this book, is typical: "Bibliothèque happened by default," explains founding partner Mason Wells. "The decision to start our own business was creative and not financial. The three of us had worked at our previous studios (Jon Jeffrey at Farrow, and Tim Beard and me at North) for about eight years and things were beginning to stagnate. No matter how much creativity you assert, you still have to answer to somebody else. This general frustration at the lack of control became a catalyst to just get on with it. Needless to say, our frustrations became a positive energy and the business evolved."

"Between the three of us," he continues, "we had ideas that just didn't fit into the framework of our previous jobs. Now we have control and it's incredibly liberating. We work differently and we don't have to answer to anyone but ourselves. It's a far more organic process, allowing us to control every aspect of the job, every step of the way. A year down the line we have worked on jobs we would never have dreamt about. We have built up an excellent client roster and have attained financial stability beyond our previous jobs. Most importantly though, starting Bibliothèque has rekindled our passion for design."

Designers start studios for many reasons. They do it because they reach an age when an inner voice tells them to take control of their creative and financial destinies. They do it when they realize they don't want to spend the rest of their lives working for someone else, or when they think they can do it better than the person who currently employs them. The trigger might be the sudden appearance of a client that makes setting up a studio feasible. It could even be the meeting of a kindred spirit who is seen as a likely business partner.

This brings us neatly to the first golden rule of forming a studio: find a partner or partners. It's a rare designer who is able to set up and run a studio with themselves as sole proprietor in charge of a team of people. There are designers who do it, but like mountaineers climbing Everest in swimwear, you don't see it often.

## Business partnerships

Once you've decided that having a business partner—or partners—is a good idea, all you have to do is find the right person or persons. You don't have to choose close friends (separate lives away from the studio can be beneficial), but you must choose people that you can talk to frankly and unguardedly. From time to time you and your partners will be required to open yourselves up to intense personal scrutiny from each other. So choose carefully: going into business with the wrong people can be expensive and emotionally damaging. You will never find partners who share your every view—and in truth, a degree of healthy diversity is desirable. But you need to share broad principles; if you don't, conflict will inevitably arise. There needs to be at least some common ground, both creatively (the sort of work the studio is going to do and an overall policy relating to creative direction), and in the way you intend to conduct your business (business ethics and how you treat staff, suppliers, and the people you come into contact with).

Even when you have formed a good business partnership, the hard work is only just beginning. Partnerships have to be tended, nurtured, and repaired when damaged. In the early days, when you are high on the buzz of running your own studio, relationships don't need much tending—you are too busy to worry about them. But when times are hard and money is scarce, business partners start to question each other's worth and to detect real or imagined signs of inequality and unfairness. And remember, people change, and those ideals that you all signed up to at the beginning aren't necessarily the same ones you'll rally round in five to ten years' time. So, be flexible and be prepared for changes in yourself and in others.

Partnerships also need to be protected by written agreements: emotional chemistry isn't enough. A directors' agreement, drawn up by a lawyer, is an important safeguard and a legal requirement in many countries. It may go against the spirit of communal endeavor in which your business was forged, but a legally binding exit strategy is mandatory. During the first thirteen years of Intro, I never once contemplated leaving. (My wife often said that she wished she were one of my clients: "Then I'd see more of you.") But at some indefinable point I changed, and I realized I wanted to leave and do other things. Without directors' agreements in place, this exit might have been complicated and rancorous. It wasn't.

**How to be a graphic designer, without losing your soul**

Partnerships don't have to be equal. It is possible to have unequal shareholdings, distributed among two or more partners. This is a highly charged area with great potential for unhappiness and dissatisfaction. You will need to take careful advice on this aspect of your relationship. It is difficult to change the share structure of companies once they are in place. Tread cautiously and listen carefully to the advice you are given. Challenge anything that doesn't feel correct or fair, but whatever you do, don't start off with the wrong partnership structure.

[4] For British readers, here is a link to a government site that advises on legal structures for businesses in the UK. www.businesslink. gov.uk

From *On Design and Innovation: A selection of lectures organized by the Royal Society for the Encouragement of Arts, Manufactures and Commerce,* [5] Gower, 1999.

In his lecture "Tomato —A New Model for Creative Enterprise," delivered to the Royal Society of Arts, Tomato's managing director Steve Baker said: "I have often been motivated by seeing frustrated potential and have for a long time thought that most creative people have extreme difficulty in exploiting their own talents. Many of them have tremendous problems [6] handling money and sometimes get embarrassed just by having to talk about it. They usually undersell themselves or occasionally go to the opposite extreme, pricing themselves out of the market, and become impossible to trade with." From *On Design and Innovation,* 1999.

Having eulogized the benefits of partnerships, it must be acknowledged that there are other fiscal models for running design groups. To discover which is the best legal framework for you, you need to study them all and decide which fits your circumstances. There are online guides that will help you decide which is right for you. [4]

Steve Baker of Tomato describes the collectivist nature of the celebrated London company: "Tomato acts very much like an agency, negotiating fees, invoicing and chasing for payment, and retaining a percentage before paying through to the individuals concerned. Much of the way that Tomato works is based on trust. There is no need for complicated written agreements between ourselves, and our shareholders agreement, which we have to have by law, includes such phrases as 'enlightened self-interest' and 'love.' This is clearly an unconventional way of doing business and I am often faced with the blank stares of people who just don't get it." [5]

I've probably made the business of finding and choosing business partners sound more complicated, and risky, than it really is. In practice, most people manage it comfortably. In many cases, designers choose partners that they have already worked with. This makes sense, since they have already proved to each other that they can function as a team.

Good and bad at business

There is a widespread misapprehension that designers make poor businesspeople. There are even designers who think they will be better designers if they are useless at business. Business and administration are anathema to many designers, but there is not much to be gained from being willfully bad at it. [6] In fact, designers are often good at business, and many studios are paradigms of efficiency and progressive practice. But if cash flow, sales projections, negotiating with the bank, or dealing with tax officials fills you with fear and loathing, you will need help. Someone needs to take responsibility for day-to-day financial affairs, and with that comes a serious responsibility. This person must be trustworthy, open, and accountable. When you start to make money you can employ an in-house bookkeeper to help, but until then you or one of your partners will have to do it.

The much-admired designers Non-Format have a reputation for highly individualistic and visually rich work. Looking at their elegant typographic handiwork, it's easy to imagine them indulging in creativity to the point of total immersion. Yet they have a pragmatic approach to the financial management of their studio: "I actually quite enjoy the financial side of things," notes partner Jon Forss. "I put together a pretty tight system when we started so that we'd avoid a situation where, for example, we might end up with a pile of receipts and no idea what they were for. So long as everything is put into the right folder straight away, keeping track of invoices and expenses is quite easy. What makes things easiest of all, though, is that we have a firm of accountants that handle the end-of-year accounts and make sure we pay our VAT (sales tax) bill. They cost a little money each year, but we figure it's well worth it."[7]

7   From an interview in Tony Brook and Adrian Shaughnessy (eds), *Studio Culture*, Unit Editions, 2009.

To ensure efficiency, partners should each take responsibility for different areas of their business. This allocation of responsibilities allows companies to grow and function without the partners treading on each other's toes. It doesn't mean that you stop sharing decision-making. Nor does it mean there is no overlap. On the contrary, when a studio is fighting to get itself off the ground everyone must be prepared to do whatever is most pressing. But life will be easier if each partner takes ultimate responsibility for a particular area. For example, if there are three in the partnership, you might choose to allocate your responsibilities as follows (other formulations are, of course, possible):

Partner 1   Creative direction, clients, new business, promotion, and publicity
Partner 2   Financial and fiscal affairs, job costing, staff matters, health and safety
Partner 3   Production, project management, studio management, IT, and green policy

If, for example, a studio computer expires and needs to be replaced, Partner 3 should deal with it. He or she needs to decide the type of new machine required, and liaises with Partner 2 about the cost. Partner 1 is then informed of their decision, and if all three are in agreement, Partner 3 orders the new machine and takes responsibility for its integration into the studio. Since Partner 3 is also responsible for the company's green policy, Partner 3 must oversee the responsible and legal disposal of the redundant machine. Meanwhile, Partner 1 had better be getting some work through the door, or Partners 2 and 3 will have something to gripe about.

When each partner knows his or her responsibilities it is easy to get things done efficiently and reduces the likelihood of accusations of inactivity being leveled at each other. As you grow, you might want to look at more sophisticated management and organizational techniques, but in the early days of a studio's existence you will need simple procedures that allow you to execute assignments with maximum efficiency, and with results that you can be proud of.

**How to be a graphic designer, without losing your soul**

The independent business turnaround specialist John Dewhirst, a former financial director of a leading design company, wrote in *Design Week* (July 24, 2003): "There are three fundamental lessons to be learned about business failure. The first is that failure is due to a lack of cash rather than a lack of reported profit (cash is a matter of fact while profit is a matter of opinion). The second is that once a business is on a trend of underperformance, there is often a rapid acceleration into crises and ultimate demise. The third is that business failure is rarely due to a sudden or unforeseen catastrophe—time and again the same shortcomings lead to decline: defects in management, inadequate financial systems and controls, overcommitments and strategic or structural deficiencies."

8

## Creating a business plan

To fund a new studio you might need to raise money. You should avoid borrowing a large amount unless you are extremely confident about your ability to generate cash to repay the loan. It is much better, if possible, to use available cash to fund initial purchases. One of the great joys of establishing a graphic design studio is that it doesn't take vast amounts of money to get started. You need a computer, some software, a printer, a scanner, and a place to work. You will also need a good broadband Internet connection, and a supply of stimulants (caffeine or other) to keep you awake at night as you do the obligatory all-nighters.

Yet even this modest outlay shouldn't be underestimated. If there are two or three of you, you need to multiply the costs accordingly. If you have no alternative but to borrow money from a bank you will need a business plan. Even if you don't need funding, prepare a business plan anyway. It is only by doing an accurate calculation—projected income against projected expenditure with ample contingencies for the unforeseen—that you will know what you have to do to survive. But business plans are only any good if they are ruthlessly honest. You must assume the worst. Be tough on yourself, and assume that bad things will happen.8 Assume you will have more outgoings than income; assume you will have fewer clients than you hoped for; assume that you will be paid more slowly than you'd like; assume that you will have at least one bad debt in your first year. Not deceiving yourself is the secret of business planning. If you are realistic and pragmatic in the running of your business, you can afford to be cavalier in your creative life.

A good accountant can prepare a business plan for you, but try to do it yourself and get an accountant to check it. You can get help with business plans from a number of commercial and government agencies. The latter provide instructions on how to compile a business plan—and they are free.

## Professional advisers and services

You will almost certainly already have a bank account and there are advantages (and disadvantages) in sticking with an institution that already knows you. Of course, a business account is different from a personal one, and to open a business account you need to speak to a bank manager. Ask friends and fellow designers to recommend someone; arrange to meet a few managers before deciding which bank suits you. The days of feeling small and insignificant in the face of your bank manager are over. Bank managers are part of the service sector and they want your business.

Most banks have helpful start-up packs for new businesses, and a good manager will guide you through the first steps of launching a business—if he or she doesn't, ditch them and find one who will.

For the fledgling design company, having a good accountant is like having a good psychoanalyst. It is also a legal requirement that an incorporated company submits professionally accredited accounts, so there's no doing without an accountant. The main benefit, though, is having someone to talk to and someone who will listen to you about business concerns. A good accountant should save you more money than his or her services cost. Ask around and get friends to recommend some names. You need someone who will be friendly but ruthlessly dispassionate. You need someone who will always tell you the truth, even when it hurts. You also need someone who will not be patronizing. An accountant who treats you like an idiot is no use. And don't be intimidated by him or her. Ask how much they charge, and when they charge (accountants sometimes bill annually). Ask if you can speak to one or two of their existing clients for a reference (if they say no, be suspicious), and get them to say exactly what they will do for you.

You will also need a lawyer. With any luck you will speak to your lawyer only rarely. Speaking to lawyers is expensive and we tend to do it only when it is unavoidable—a lease, a contract with a client or major supplier, employment agreements. You find lawyers in exactly the same way you find an accountant—there's no truth whatsoever in the nostrum that you find lawyers by poking sticks into cracks in rocks; this is an untruth spread by people with a low opinion of the legal profession.

## Setting up

You've found a partner—or partners—and you've negotiated a partnership agreement. You've made a business plan. You've found a bank, and you've got an accountant. Having done all this, you'd have thought you could now start earning a living and doing what you do best—designing. Not yet; first you have some practical matters to take care of. Your accountant will tell you what these are, and how and when to do them, but it's worth looking at a list of the most important things you need to do to launch a company.

| | |
|---|---|
| 1 | Register your business with the relevant authorities |
| 2 | Register your company name and secure a URL |
| 3 | Set up relevant payroll and tax status |
| 4 | Issue employment contracts to staff |
| 5 | Create Terms and Conditions to be given to clients |

Amanda Merron is a partner in accountancy firm Willott Kingston Smith: she has numerous design and media-related clients and regularly offers guidance in the pages of *Design Week*. I've always found her advice to be coherent and helpful. All accountants should be this good. I asked her for her key recommendations for setting up a studio. She suggests having a clear focus on what the business offers and how it can be effectively delivered. This knowledge will go a long way toward ensuring success in a design business. When it comes to managing your finances, she points out that there are three main areas:

**How to be a graphic designer, without losing your soul**

### 1    Planning

Business planning and budgeting is often seen as a difficult, even scary, process that only accountants can tackle. This is far from the case. It is simply saying what you think is likely to happen in terms of cost and income, and writing it down. This is not an exact process—in fact, the most accurate thing you can say is that it will be wrong. It makes sense to consider which of the assumptions made is most likely to change and assess the impact of that.

### 2    Reporting

Having written a sensible plan, actual business performance should be measured against what you thought was going to happen. Trying to measure performance in isolation is practically impossible. Is an income of $100,000 for the year good? Not if you expected $200,000, but if you had only planned for $75,000 you might be pleased. What should be reported? Key elements are as follows:

|  | Plan $ | Actual $ | Difference $ |
|---|---|---|---|
| Fee income | 100,000 | 80,000 | (20,000) |
| Cost | (50,000) | (50,000) | – |
| Profit | 50,000 | 30,000 | (20,000) |
| Bank balance | 40,000 | 20,000 | (20,000) |

As well as looking back to see what happened, it is vital to look forward to consider what new work might be coming in, how much cash is likely to be needed, and so on, on a regular basis.

### 3    Reacting

Any significant deviation from the plan should be investigated and something should be done about it. For example, if income is lower than anticipated, can you raise your fees or cut costs somewhere?

### Finding premises

If you have the space, you might start off by working from home. Even if you haven't got the space, consider working from home anyway; set up in your bedroom, your garage, your garden shed, or your kitchen until you have some income flowing in the direction of your bank account. Only then should you consider acquiring premises, or staff, or that Gaggia coffee machine. Most clients won't mind you working from home; they can be surprisingly generous and supportive toward start-ups and often like to be seen to be helping young design teams get started—especially if they think they are going to be cheaper than established companies. Anyway, as long as you are prepared to visit them every time they want a meeting, they needn't know where you're based. In the new networked world, we can be anywhere we want to be.

But at some point you will want to find premises that enable you to set up a proper studio. A good way to start is by talking to other designers, especially designers who already rent space. They will sometimes know of opportunities that are available via their existing landlords. Also, larger studios sometimes sublet space. Again, this will do while you are getting your studio established, but as you grow, a cuckoo-like existence within another studio will feel unsatisfactory, and you will want to move on. There's a scene in Dave Eggers' book *A Heartbreaking Work of Staggering Genius* that many designers will find familiar. Eggers describes the hassles of renting studio space in which to produce a magazine. In doing so, he offers another sort of arrangement (a slightly eccentric one, it must be said) for a graphic design start-up: "We move our offices from our condemned warehouse to the fifth floor of a glassy office box in the middle of the city. The [San Francisco] *Chronicle* promotions department, wanting us close so Moodie and I can provide lightning-quick service, have let us move in with them … giving us about 800 square feet, with floor-to-ceiling windows, for $1,000 a month—which Moodie and I easily pay by overcharging them for our design work." These arrangements can work well, but tolerance is soon exhausted, and disgruntlement can quickly set in. And be wary of following Eggers' fictional example and overcharging: this tactic has a way of coming back to bite you.

How do you know how much space to rent? Ask designer friends who run their own studios. Go and visit small studios and get a feel for space in relation to number of bodies. Once you've established a good people-to-space ratio, make do with less space than you'd like: you won't mind being cramped for the first few months. Take a short lease so that you can walk away if everything goes wrong, or so that you can trade up if you start to do well.

Making friends—rather than enemies—with the people you encounter in professional life is a good policy. At Intro, we started life in a tiny office at the top of a large building. The rooms weren't smart, but they were adequate for our first eighteen months. At the end of our tenancy we had plenty of work, a steady income, and good prospects (it was a boom time in the UK for design), and we felt confident enough to rent a large building on five floors in central London. The rent was hefty, but if we carried on doing as well as we had been we could cover it comfortably. And for a year or so, we did. We enjoyed having a large building that allowed everyone plenty of space, and gave us, as a company, a bit of swagger. Big mistake. We hit the economic downturn of the early 1990s with a Titanic-like thump. Our income shrank, and we found ourselves with a rent that we could barely cope with.

But we had a lifeline. The young real estate agent who we had hired to find the building for us had become a friend. We were one of his first transactions; he was ambitious and dynamic and had taken a shine to us. We approached him for help. He went to the building's owners and negotiated a reduced rent on our behalf. He did this because we'd treated him with respect during the transaction (he could also see that we were a serious and ambitious group of people who would doubtless make another move soon, and when we did we'd award him the task of finding a new office for us). Don't rely on this happening if you get into trouble; acts of disinterested kindness are rare in business, and even rarer in the world of real estate. We had a lucky break, and without it we might not have survived. But the reason we got lucky was because we'd made a friend of our agent. Friends are better than enemies is the only lesson here.

**How to be a graphic designer, without losing your soul**

Choosing a name

You've made your move. You've set up on your own. You've acquired enough computer kit to compete with NASA (your accountant advised you on whether to buy or lease), and you've secured premises (they are next door to a twenty-four-hour pizza parlor, and there was a guy asleep on your doorstep this morning clutching a bottle of something that smelled like lighter fuel mixed with urine, but it's your studio and you love it). Now you must choose a name. Fashions in design group names change constantly. I can't offer much advice here other than to remind you that you will have to live with your chosen name for a long time. In years to come you might change the nature of your business, so you don't want to be sad-dled with a name that is inappropriate. It's worth remembering also that names pass into a sort of neutrality after a while. Like a new pair of shoes, a new name feels stiff and conspicu-ous to start with, but just as you "grow into" new shoes and they become part of your skin, so too with names. Unless, of course, you choose something really stupid.

Identity

Once you've got your name, you must start work on a studio identity. Dragging a grand piano up Everest with your teeth will be easier, but you've got to do it. Few things will vex you quite as much as creating your studio's identity. It exposes a weakness in the mentality of most designers: we are generally bad at designing for ourselves. Designers spend their working lives telling their clients how to cultivate an appropriate image, yet often seem paralyzed when they have to do the same for themselves. It doubtless has to do with the deep-seated notion that to be a designer you need a brief. But short of inviting another design company to design your identity, you have to get on with it, and you have to do it well. The best way to do this is to treat it like a job from a client. Agree among yourselves who is going to do it, then write a proper brief with objectives, schedules, and budgets, and make it into a real live job. When it's done, assess the results with detachment and objectivity. In fact, do everything that you would do with an external job, except send yourself a bill.

Conclusion

The three most important watchwords for working life are: impermanence, speed, and reinvention. Those who grasp these concepts and learn to deal with them will find working life less arduous than those who fail or refuse to accept them. It seems to me that designers, with their gift for unfettered thinking and adventurousness, are well suited to this new world order where nothing stays the same, where everything moves at dizzying speed, and where we may need to professionally reinvent ourselves on more than one occasion throughout a working lifetime. Of course, there are other watchwords for contemporary life and work: ethics, creativity, and reliability. If we can retain these quali-ties, we will cope with life as a designer no matter whether we live a nomadic freelance existence or establish a studio.

Running a studio How do you know when to employ more staff? / employing creative staff / hanging onto creative staff / spotting talent / non-design staff / account handlers / studio systems / studio philosophy. Examination of the main business and creative aspects of running a design studio. Or how to be a progressive employer.

**How to be a graphic designer, without losing your soul**

In the early days of a studio, when we are under pressure to become established or to at least get a foothold on the road to survival, it feels as if we are ricocheting between extremes: creativity or profitability; freedom or compromise; stasis or growth; the individual or the group; survival or failure. But one of the first lessons we learn about running a studio is that the dualisms listed above are not choices, but parts of a daily negotiation that we have to enter into. How we conduct these "negotiations" determines the way our studio develops.

What do I mean by this? Let's look at the words "stasis" and "growth." In the context of a design studio, stasis appears to mean staying the same, not changing, not taking risks. Growth, on the other hand, seems to entail expansion, radical change, and risk-taking. But when we look at what studio life is really like we see that these two concepts are not quite what they seem. For example, it is actually not possible for a business to stand still. As all the business gurus point out, companies only have two gears, forward and reverse, and standing still is the same as going backward. So, even if our goal is to stay small, we have to be proactive and work at it. In fact, in a changing world, we have to grow to stand still.

The great Tibor Kalman got it right when he said: "The toughest thing when running a studio is not to grow." What Kalman meant was that any studio that is any good will attract more work than it can cope with, and when this happens, choices have to be made. It doesn't mean we have to abandon our principles or our commitment to smallness. Nor does it mean that we have to rush headlong into growth. It does mean that we have to negotiate a path that allows us to balance competing needs—it won't happen automatically. We only achieve goals in life by negotiating our way toward them: bulldozing our way doesn't work. The most important skill needed to run a studio is a questioning sensibility.

In the following pages we will look at some of the numerous questions and challenges facing studio heads.

How do you know when to employ more staff?

In the early days of running my studio (when there were only four or five of us), I did many different jobs: from changing light bulbs and unblocking toilets to convincing grim-faced CEOs that our fledgling studio with its sparse portfolio of work was worth hiring. I stayed up all night designing album covers for stroppy record labels that sent copy in at 9.00pm and wanted finished artwork twelve hours later. I was even threatened with violence by an enraged window cleaner (I mention this only to make the point that when you start up a design company you have to do anything and everything—even deal with emotionally unstable window cleaners).

Most design studios start like this: we do everything ourselves until we can afford some help. But as part of the ongoing "negotiations" mentioned above, there may come a time when we decide that we need more people. This is a matter of careful judgement. We don't want to employ people if we don't have any work for them. Similarly, we don't want to expire from overwork ourselves, or lose opportunities to take on new and interesting clients because we are understaffed. Furthermore, if we try to do everything ourselves (which is the right thing to do when starting out), we will not only become exhausted, but we will start to produce sub-standard work, and will inevitably lose clients. Employing new people at key moments (even if it is only one person a year) will allow controlled development; failure to do so will mean, at best, that we don't have enough help to run our studio, and at worse that we run the risk of staying permanently in neutral gear.

Early on at Intro, our policy was to recruit only when we had a steady flow of guaranteed work. This was fine as a start-up policy, but since, as I've already noted, new designers can take time to bed in, it was only partially successful as a strategy. After a while, when we had grown in confidence and our financial situation had improved, we took on staff ahead of anticipated need. This gave us some breathing space to get new staff acclimatized.

To bring in new staff without careful financial planning, and without the confidence that we will generate enough work for them, is dangerous. But here's something that might surprise you: every time I employed someone—especially if they were brimming with potential—it raised my game. By this sporting metaphor I mean that I became more confident and more determined, with the consequence that I became better at winning new work and better at promoting our studio. So, rather than being a dampener or a self-canceling strain on the business, a new person was actually a catalyst for improvement. It's hard to quantify or measure this effect, but it worked every time.

## Employing creative staff

In Chapter 1 I looked at how tough it is for the new designer to find a job, but spare a moment for the poor employer: it is just as tough finding good employees. Getting the right people—partners, design staff, non-design staff—is the one thing a start-up design studio can't afford to get wrong. It's possible to screw up in every other area and still prosper, but in recruitment we can't afford to make mistakes. In this chapter I'll look at ways to find, assess, and secure talent. And then I'll discuss how to treat the people we work with, because it is not enough to find and hire talented people; we have to nurture them too.

When I co-founded Intro, I discounted most of the advice I was given by well-meaning acquaintances and businesspeople, because I wanted to trust my common sense and intuition. I wanted to find new and fresh ways of doing things, and I figured that if I listened to everything I was told I'd end up adopting a lot of old-fashioned formulaic thinking. I also felt that "design was different." and I was loathe to take guidance from anyone who didn't know about the quirks and slightly wonky logic of the design world. Of course, I was more arrogant than I am now, and wrongly imagined that I didn't need the help of outsiders.

However, one piece of advice that I was offered struck me as perversely good. In fact, so good that much later I found it to be the single most helpful piece of advice anyone gave me concerning the running of a design studio. It came from an unlikely source, too—an acquaintance who had made numerous attempts to become a successful businessman, all of which had ended in failure, and who knew nothing about design or designers. He told me: "Always employ people who are better than you."

At a critical stage in the development of Intro, we experimented with a management consultant: he advised a course of restructuring that didn't seem to fit into our flatter, more democratic structure. I asked him why he'd recommended this approach. He looked miffed, and replied: "Well, because it's what everyone else does." Bad answer. Needless to say, we didn't take his advice, and after he showed us an "instructional" video that used McDonald's corporate practices as its basis, we decided not to retain his services.

# How to be a graphic designer, without losing your soul

Did the earth move for you when you read this? It didn't for me when I first heard it, although it was eventually to become my first rule of creative recruitment. I suspect for designers, perhaps recruiting for the first time in their careers, it is tough advice to swallow. Designers are a vulnerable breed; easily discouraged, easily damaged, and quick to feel threatened. Not many designers willingly agree to be upstaged by new talent in their own backyard. I wrestled with this notion for a long time before finding the courage to put it into practice. But as soon as I did, I saw it for the great truism it is. When I witnessed the benefits of employing designers more talented than myself, I was able to concentrate on the things I did best (creative direction and working with clients).

Now, I'm aware that formulations like "better than" are largely redundant in design. What does it mean if you say that someone is a "better designer" than someone else? To have any meaning it would have to be accompanied by caveats and elaborate qualifiers. But what my well-intentioned advice-giver meant was that employing people who have skills and abilities that you lack is the only way to ensure a studio's growth and development. It allows you to offer more to clients, and it allows you to delegate some of the tasks you've been struggling to perform, enabling you to concentrate on the things that you do best.

This brings us to the second rule of creative recruitment. This harsh-sounding rule states that any employee who is any good will leave. Now, on the surface, this is not good news: who wants to employ people if they are going to move on? Yet the notion of departing talent has a hidden benefit: because the departure of talent is inevitable, we are obliged to operate a perpetual search for fresh talent. Employers and studio heads tend to interview prospective employees only when they need to. This is short-sighted. It is a good idea to instigate a regular program of portfolio viewing. Try to see two or three people each month. You will need to be frank with your interviewees and state that you have agreed to see them because you are "planning ahead;" and you need to tell your existing staff, who may feel threatened by the regularity with which you view the work of other designers, that it is your policy to constantly view portfolios. It is one of the ways you future-proof your studio.

This brings me to another rule of creative recruitment, this time given to me by a successful businessman friend. Like the advice from my less successful acquaintance, it seemed to sneer at common sense. This is what he told me: "People who want to have their own businesses make the best employees. Never be frightened to employ people who ultimately want to start their own studios. Think about it," he said, "it's what you did." [2]

2 My adviser gave me another dollop of wisdom that I was less enamored with. He told me to "only employ people who are married with children and mortgages—they are more reliable. Less likely to upset the apple cart." I like people who upset apple carts, I ignored this advice.

There are other aspects to departing staff that we need to be aware of. Former staff can poach clients; clients can choose to follow former employees; ex-employees can claim credit for work that wasn't done by them, or where they only played a minor role[3]; former employees can set up rival studios and compete directly with us.

Some of the above—such as poaching clients and setting up in competition—can be dealt with by employment contracts. These are essential and unavoidable in the modern workplace. But in reality, there isn't much we can do to stop an ex-employee from behaving badly. One of the best ways of dealing with these matters is to treat everyone as generously as possible, and to always live with the realization that our favorite employee might one day become our business rival. By accepting this, by building it into our thinking and planning, we reduce the likelihood of surprise and bitterness when it happens.

### Hanging onto creative staff

Losing staff may be inevitable, but I'm not advocating complacency. There are many things we can do to reduce the risk of losing key people: we can pay better salaries than other studios; we can offer better benefits and more congenial working conditions; we can offer key staff members equity in our company. Financial benefits such as these need to be planned carefully, and should be part of an overall financial plan for the company. It is advisable to have the help of an accountant here. Employing staff is a bit like having children. Suddenly, we have to become less selfish.

Our commitment to staff doesn't end with fiscal matters. The most important thing we can offer a designer is good work. This will override most feelings of restlessness, even if it sometimes means that we have to take on work that is not profitable, but that offers designers a chance to create the sort of work they want to do.

There are other ways to demonstrate our commitment to staff. For instance, it is sometimes necessary to back an individual designer at the expense of a client. If a client is being unreasonable, and if the designer has done everything within his or her powers to ensure a satisfactory outcome, then we must back the designer and sack the client. I've done this on a number of occasions and designers recognize the sacrifice that has been made and repay the gesture with renewed energy and commitment.[4] Naturally, we need to be careful here; if we start sacking clients every time they upset a member of our design team, we will have no business left. But a bad client can cause as much damage as a good one can bring benefits. Knowing when to sack a client is a matter of careful judgement.

3 Erik Spiekermann once said in an interview: "I've seen portfolios that people have presented to me containing work done by me. They weren't even there. Forgery has become so easy, so if you give somebody a credit, it's out in the open." From Tony Brook and Adrian Shaughnessy (eds), *Studio Culture*, Unit Editions, 2009.

4 I once sacked a client whose behavior toward one of our designers was unreasonable. When I told the designer what I'd done, she begged me to change my mind and said that she didn't mind having her life made miserable after all. From then on I always checked with the designer before sacking a client.

**How to be a graphic designer, without losing your soul**

Is there anything less drastic we can do to show commitment to our designers? At Intro, we allowed designers to have personal credits on the work they produced, and made sure they were name-checked when the company's work was featured in magazines. Encouraging designers to sign their work (a typical credit would read: Designed by Jo Smith, Intro) flies in the face of conventional wisdom, which states that you keep your designers hidden, that you should only ever promote the firm's brand name and never allow employees to develop a profile. But personal credits on work and citations in the design press create loyalty and openness. Through the implementation of this simple device, designers are able to achieve peer recognition and derive a sense of personal authorship— as well as having documentary evidence of their contributions, and something to show their mothers.

This policy of encouraging personal credits has to be balanced by the fact that a great many design projects are jointly authored; many individuals—designers and non-designers—may contribute to a project's success. As a precaution, I retained the right to change a credit if I felt it was unmerited. In practice, I never had to do this.

## Spotting talent

When you interview a designer you are looking for three things: talent, suitability, and potential. How do you spot these qualities? Intuition and experience play a big part, but perhaps the best way to learn to spot desirable qualities is to make a few mistakes. I was once asked by a British design school to set a project for the students. In a fit of generosity (we were doing well), I said that I'd offer the winner a period of paid employment. When the results came through, there were two astonishing pieces of work with nothing to choose between either. I found myself with two winners. I interviewed the two students, and I ended up hiring both of them (as I said, we really were doing well at the time).

One of the two proved to be an able and talented individual who stayed with us for a number of years; the other was a disaster and had to be asked to leave at the end of his first week. I had been seduced by his work, and I'd forgotten to properly assess his character. The point I'm making here is that we have to look for signs beyond the pages of designers' portfolios. We can take references from previous employers, though this is not so easy in the case of recent graduates where we have to rely on intuition. But nothing sharpens up our judgement like an expensive mistake.

It's also worth noting that talent will find you. Good designers only approach good studios; anyone with any talent is only going to be attracted to a studio or a firm with a good reputation. If you have a good reputation, talent will find you.

## Non-design staff

Employing non-creative staff (administrators, studio managers, receptionists, project managers, producers) is just like employing creative staff: we choose people who are sympathetic to the culture of our studios. But we only start to think about employing non-design staff once we've grown to a size where our workload is threatening to overwhelm us, and where it has become economically viable to employ people who are not, primarily, fee-generating.

At Intro, I was initially resistant to employing non-designers; I couldn't see the logic of employing non-fee-generating people. Surely it would reduce our profitability? In fact, thanks to my business partner's perceptiveness, the improved efficiency that came from employing talented and able support staff meant that more work was done (with no drop in quality) and more income was generated.

Almost certainly, a bookkeeper should be your first non-creative appointment. Next, you might think about a project manager, or studio manager, or a production person. Employing someone with project-management skills can free designers from administrative, production, and financial chores. The studio model we built at Intro was as follows: small teams of designers led by a senior designer and each team supported by a project manager. I was resistant to this formula at first. I'd always done my own production—liaised with printers, budgeted jobs, negotiated with clients—and I believed that it made designers stronger if they had this experience. I still believe that designers, in the early stages of their careers, benefit from having to do their own production and administration—but it's doubtful whether many of them are much good at it, and the benefits of partnering designers with project managers are unquestionable.

Project managers—or a studio manager—should take control of all production matters relating to a job (helping with presentations, preparing costings, negotiating budgets, controlling paperwork, scheduling, monitoring progress, dealing with external suppliers, invoicing, and remembering to charge for extras—something designers notoriously forget to do). This is also a good way to deal with difficult clients. Project managers can have those prickly conversations with clients about budgets, delayed schedules, and payment wrangles, leaving designers free to talk about the project at hand.

The businessman Ricardo Semler, who turned his Brazilian company Semco into a blueprint for egalitarian and progressive working practices, wrote in his book *Maverick!*: "We don't have receptionists. We don't think they are necessary, despite all our visitors. We don't have secretaries either, or personal assistants. We don't believe in cluttering the payroll with ungratifying, dead-end jobs. Everyone at Semco, even top managers, fetches guests, stands over photocopiers, sends faxes, types letters, and dials the phones … It's all part of running a 'natural business.'"

Semler is on to something: dead-end jobs breed dead-end attitudes. The idea that a studio should employ someone to do the stuff that no one else wants to do is self defeating. But it still means that tasks such as answering the phone quickly and in a friendly manner; welcoming studio visitors and arranging basic hospitality; ordering couriers and making parcels, have to be done by existing staff.

Adding non-design staff alters the dynamics of a studio. It might enable us to do more work, but it adds to our financial overhead and makes it imperative to increase our turnover. This might mean losing some freedom: the freedom to turn away uncongenial work, for instance. But it might also mean the opportunity to take on some of the work we see being done by larger studios and that makes us think *I can do that*. I would also add that, in my experience, once we had taken the decision to hire non-designers, I enjoyed a new-found sanity that—despite the need to increase our income—freed me to do what I did best. This is one of the great paradoxes of studio life, and it is what I mean when I say that running a studio is a constant negotiation with competing demands.

**How to be a graphic designer, without losing your soul**

## Account handlers

I've never been a fan of the idea of account handlers. I'm sure there are good ones, and I know there are clients who will pay handsomely to have a dedicated account handler looking after them. But I see the problems caused by account handlers when I deal with advertising agencies. I've worked on projects with creative teams in agencies, and watched as work is handed over to an account handler to be presented to the client. Since he or she has no personal investment in the work they show, if the client doesn't like the work they have less incentive to defend it. They simply bring it back like a dog with a bone and deposit it at the feet of the creative team and say, "rejected." Account handlers also have the effect of making designers feel dislocated from the design process. Client contact is essential if designers are going to do meaningful work. I've always believed in exposing even novice designers to clients; few things make a designer mature more quickly than lots of client contact.

I've already noted how beneficial it can be for designers to be removed from the direct responsibility of negotiating with clients over money and scheduling, by the introduction of a good project manager or production person, but when a designer loses direct contact with the client he or she simply becomes less effective and less committed.

## Studio systems

Designers are often resistant to excessive bureaucracy. Quite right too. If your day is spent filling in timesheets and other dreary administrative tasks, you won't have much time or appetite for creative work. But it is another paradox in the life of a designer that we are at our most free when we are at our most organized.

I found this great quote by the eminent British architect Sir Hugh Casson: "The belief has been allowed to grow up that good art and good administration are incompatible. A good designer to many people means an architect who cannot be trusted to keep a budget or a program. An able administrator implies ignorance of or indifference to visual matters. Neither charge is wholly untrue. Neither does the profession credit. Both undermine the architect's claim to be the leader of the (…) team."[5] If we substitute the word "architect" with the words "graphic designer," Casson's words (written in 1972) apply today.

It also explains why designers are not always trusted by their clients, and why designers often sit in lowly positions in the creative food chain. We can rise up this chain by improving our administration skills. For designers with an aversion to admin, there is a solution: a project manager (or producer, or studio manager). These are wonderful individuals—visionary individuals—with the god-like skill of organization. However, until we can afford one of these admin deities (they can often be hired part-time), it is essential that we undertake the basic requirements of organization ourselves.

5   From Robert Green, *The Architect's Guide to Running a Job*, Architectural Press, 1972.

Here's a list of what needs to be done to keep track of work, costs, and income. Studios need systems to deal with the following:

1. Booking in and logging work
2. Securing client purchase orders or project contracts
3. Scheduling projects and monitoring workflow
4. Logging and allocating costs
5. Monitoring cash flow, which includes debt-chasing
6. Paying salaries, suppliers, and rent
7. Ordering studio supplies (computers, software, tea/coffee)
8. Maintaining IT network with software for administration and accounting support

Studio philosophy

As well as good people and good work, studios need to have a philosophy; or, to put it another way, studios need to have something they can believe in. My "philosophy" at Intro was to always try to do great work regardless of the budget and to start every project with the conviction that there was no such thing as a bad job. This meant that we did low-budget work, and work that appeared on the surface to have not much potential, with the same enthusiasm and commitment that we applied to big-budget work with a sexy brief.

Not a terribly grand or noble philosophy, I admit, but it was something the whole studio believed in, and it was something that we could shout about and tell our clients about without sounding like creeps.

We also allowed our designers to pursue their own creative vision, and resisted the temptation to impose a studio straitjacket on them. In other words, there was no house style. Designers were free to be themselves creatively, with only one proviso: there had to be clients who wanted what they did. By encouraging our designers to "be themselves," clients got striking and individualistic design while we had the benefit of designers who felt liberated and respected for what they did best.[6] This notion of respect, and allowing each individual the maximum amount of freedom, extended to non-design staff. It was fundamental to the way we approached creative and business life and was woven into the fabric of the company.

6 This philosophy sometimes made promoting Intro difficult. Trying to attract new clients with so many stylistic and conceptual voices on offer wasn't always easy. I often looked at studios and indviduals with a consistent style and envied them. Surely their lives were much easier than ours, I thought. With us, clients weren't sure what they were being offered—although, it has to be said, some clients loved this fact about us.

# How to be a graphic designer, without losing your soul

There are, of course, other types of "philosophy." Many designers believe in schools of design that come with inbuilt notions of ethical conduct. Modernism, for example, with its high moral tone of rationality and truthfulness; "protest design," with its political and campaigning function; "design for social good," with its rejection of purely financial motives in favor of design that benefits society. Others believe in sustainable design practices: "green" issues such as the use of recycled materials for printing, and avoiding design that merely contributes to landfill sites,[7] are increasingly preoccupying designers. I know designers who believe passionately in the democratizing and participatory merits of interactive digital design. And I know designers who carry a sword for aesthetic standards in design.

The one thing that this book will not tell you is what your philosophy should be. That is a matter for individuals and groups to decide for themselves. Telling people how they should conduct themselves is behavioral fundamentalism, and anathema to me. The matter of ethics and social responsibility in design is dealt with in more detail in Chapter 8.

But I firmly believe that every studio needs a philosophy. We have to be prepared to stand up for this philosophy and not discard it at the first sign of trouble. If we want to be taken seriously, we have to believe in something, and that something has to be genuine; it has to be something by which we can be measured, first by ourselves and then by others. We mustn't be frightened of promulgating our beliefs. People respect principles, especially in a world where they are becoming increasingly rare.

## Conclusion

Setting up a studio in partnership with like-minded individuals and staffing it with like-minded designers and non-designers is one of the great adventures open to a designer. It is a rare designer who hasn't contemplated doing it. Intriguingly, among those who take the plunge, very few go back to paid employment after tasting the nectar of freedom; and, despite the late nights, the disappointment, the extra pressure, and the added responsibility, it really is freedom.

At first we think that having to deal with everything from the way our studios are lit (very important actually) to the way we present work to clients appears daunting—even off-putting. But when we get it right, there are few things more satisfying than the buzz that comes from running a design studio. When Experimental Jetset were asked what it meant to be part of a studio, they described it as "that magical feeling when the whole turns out to be more than the sum of its parts."[8]

7   CDs are non-biodegradable. Design studios use large quantities of these silver disks. By throwing them into landfill sites, we are creating problems for our grandchildren. There are firms that will now take discarded CDs for various recycling purposes. Their addresses can easily be found on the Internet.

8   Interview in Tony Brook and Adrian Shaughnessy (eds), *Studio Culture*, Unit Editions, 2009.

Identification of the best ways to attract good work. Or why worrying about where the next job is coming from never goes away.

**How to be a graphic designer, without losing your soul**

It is common for even the most successful design groups to have no idea what work they will be doing in six months' time. It's worse for many small studios and freelance designers, who rarely know what work they will be doing in two weeks' time, never mind six months. Even the famous designers who we imagine are never short of work have periods of drought; and very few designers—even the busiest—always get the sort of work they want. For most of us, the quest for new and better work is never-ending.

The search for work is one of the fundamentals of life as an independent graphic designer. The energy we put into designing has to be matched by the energy we put into finding new—and better—work.

But how well equipped are designers to find fresh assignments and new clients? We are rarely taught anything about the subject in design school, and few of us are given the training enjoyed by, for example, the bright-eyed photocopier sales executive who sold us that too large, underused copier that sits in the corner of our studio. Fortunately, we're not missing much—the training received by the photocopier salesperson would not be helpful to designers. In fact, for designers, when it comes to finding new clients and winning new business, most sales techniques are too imprecise, too intrusive, and too wasteful. Yet if we want to find the sort of work that inspires us, we have to present ourselves to clients in ways that make them take notice. Paradoxically, the best way to attract good work is by doing good work.

## How do clients choose designers?

When it comes to hiring a designer, numerous professional factors play a part in helping clients make a decision: portfolio, web site, track record, reputation, fees, resources, location, and existing or past clients. However, an element of personal chemistry also plays a major part in the decision-making process; generally, clients work with people they get along with. This doesn't mean that all designers have to be fun-loving social butterflies. Nor does it mean that we have to tell clients only what they want to hear or be creepy yes-sayers. Quite the opposite. It is fine to be serious-minded and uncompromising, just so long as we bring integrity and professionalism to the relationship and stick to the simple rules of human relationships: the same ones that also apply in normal social life—empathy, understanding, and tolerance.

Yet even when we boast a tool kit of interpersonal skills, a striking portfolio of work, a list of top-notch clients, and a glowing reputation, we still have to sell ourselves and our services. This is never an easy job, and it's especially difficult today when the buyer is nearly always king. As the business writers Jonas Ridderstråle and Kjell Nordström state in their book *Funky Business*: "In the surplus society the customer is more than king: the customer is the mother of all dictators. And this time it's for real. If the customer speaks you have to jump high and jump fast. The customer wants products in orange with purple spots. The customer wants them today in Fiji. You have to deliver otherwise you will soon be out of business."[1]

Jonas Ridderstråle
and Kjell Nordström,
*Funky Business: Talent
Makes Capital Dance*,
Pearson Education,
1   2000.

Finding clients

Clients are everywhere, often where we least expect them to
be. Yet it's a well-established rule of design that we rarely get
to work with the commissioners we most want to work with.
Chances are that our targets are also everyone else's targets, so it's wiser to look off the beaten track. Most clients are
found by accident or by tortuous paths that all lead back to
luck and coincidence; this is true of the big design groups as
well as smaller ones—don't let anyone tell you different.[2]

It's tempting to go after clients who already exhibit
good design sense. Think about it, though: clients who are
known for good design will know how to commission design
and therefore gravitate toward the studios *they* want to work
with. Better instead to go after companies and institutions that
need root-and-branch help. We will have to work harder, but if
we are successful the results will be infinitely more satisfying.
In my experience, there is far greater satisfaction in taking a
client with no apparent potential and producing effective and
resonant work for them than there is in working for "cool
brands" and design-savvy clients.

One of the most valuable assets that a freelance
designer or studio can acquire is a database of contacts.[3]
There are various proprietary databases available on the market that will enable us to build up a list of contacts by logging
the name and details of everyone we come into contact with.
No matter how tenuous the connection, log their details. Scan
magazines looking for suitable names and companies. Read
the job vacancy pages in newspapers: if there's a vacancy for
a marketing director to "oversee the company's image," then
we know that in a few months' time there will be a new person
trying to make a mark, and looking for bright new talent to help
him or her do it.

If we take these steps, in a remarkably short space of time we will accumulate a valuable database of contacts. These names are the future recipients of our ongoing promotional
activities. This is the magic circle of people we will keep in contact with by sending them letters,
e-mail newsletters, and mailers. But—and it's a mighty big but—we need to love that database.
We need to look at it constantly. We need to tend it carefully and make sure it is up to date. There
is nothing shabbier than contacting a person who left a post a year before, or if we get their job
title wrong, or send them the same communication twice. It shows we're behind the beat. A
database that isn't looked after is like a dog that is neglected—the lack of care shows.

2　I was once told by a
client that I had been
wooing for a number of
months that she had
decided to use another
studio. She named the
studio, a big name at
the time on the London
scene. I imagined their
sales team targeting
her with a lavish pres-
entation. But this wasn't
the case: she'd met
the studio's boss 'at a
wedding'.

3　There are laws relating
to the holding of infor-
mation on individuals.
Take advice from your
accountant or a quali-
fied adviser on this and
related matters.

**How to be a graphic designer, without losing your soul**

Sales techniques

How do we sell ourselves without looking and sounding as if we are selling dubious timeshare schemes? Big design firms have the funds to use sophisticated sales and marketing strategies. They might even have a team of people just doing "new business." They will host seminars, give lectures, publish research, write articles in the business press (as well as the design press), and maintain ultra-slick web sites. The rest of us have to rely on less sophisticated methods. We might have a web site, and from time to time (usually when we run out of work) we might send out e-mail newsletters and the occasional eye-catching mailer.[4] We might enter design competitions in the hope of being able to add the words "award-winning" to our work, and we submit projects to the design press. From time to time we might sharpen up our portfolios and ask existing or potential clients if we can show them our latest offerings. We usually only do this when we run out of work—or to put it more bluntly, when it's too late.

Here's a little pearl of wisdom someone gave me: when writing a letter of introduction, especially a letter promoting us or our company, always write the address on the envelope by hand.

[4] It is so rare to get a letter with a handwritten address that, when confronted with a pile of letters, the one with the handwritten address is the one we are most likely to open first.

Regardless of our best efforts—sophisticated or not—a huge proportion of new-business opportunities for designers are created in one of two ways: word of mouth, or random encounters in the business and social nexus that most of us live in. The simple fact is that we get most of our work from people who know us, from people who've heard good things about us, and from networking with friends and associates.

I'm not advocating sitting about doing nothing and hoping that jobs will fly in through the window: this just won't happen. We have to get up and open the window; we have to stick our heads out and shout "*I'm here!*" We have to work incessantly to exploit every lead, connection, and opportunity that comes our way.

The British designer Matt Pyke has built a global reputation for his company, Universal Everything, while working from a tiny custom-built studio in his garden in Sheffield, in the north of England. Pyke has done this with a combination of radical eye-catching work, a dynamic web site, and a shrewd approach to self-promotion. He set up Universal Everything in 2004, and from a standing start grew the company into a dynamic and thriving entity with clients all around the world. It wasn't easy. He had to quickly learn the tricks of self-promotion: "I knew that wordy e-mails and in-depth web sites are so inefficient for communicating an overview of a studio, I wanted to hit people with the diversity of my past in an instant. I e-mailed a one-sheet collage with 50 thumbnails of past work, which was sent to everyone who I could think of who knew interesting people. It was my viral six degrees of separation theory. If they liked the work, and passed it on, eventually it would land in a perfect client's inbox."[5]

From Tony Brook and Adrian Shaughnessy (eds), *Studio Culture*,
[5] Unit Editions, 2009.

Contact from a potential client with an invitation to meet should be the goal of all new-business activity. If we set out to win commissions from every approach we make, we will be disappointed and discouraged. Instead, we should make our goals to secure face-to-face meetings: to get in front of potential clients and to have at least a chance of finding out what they are looking for and what they expect from the designers they hire. But how do we attract those calls? In the following pages we'll look at some steps we can take, but ultimately we have to do what Matt Pyke did: take an energetic and considered approach to promoting ourselves and, as I've already mentioned, always do top-notch work.

### Dedicated new-business person

I've never met a designer with a studio who didn't want someone to help with the grind of finding new business. Unfortunately, people with the skills to locate new business opportunities and then convert them into paid assignments are as rare as bankers who say, "no thanks, give it to charity" to their annual bonus. This leaves most designers with no option but to find and win their own "new business." They are often very good at it—which is hardly surprising, since who is better to sell design than the designer him- or herself? The only problem is, it's a full-time job and all designers already have a full-time job: it's called being a designer.

Perhaps, therefore, the answer is not a full-time new-business person, but an "appointment setter." This is a person with a friendly manner, capable of intelligent and diligent research, and possessing the knack of contacting potential clients and getting them to agree to meetings. It would be a big studio that could afford a full-time appointment setter, but it is often possible to hire a part-time appointment setter, or hire someone who can perform other administrative functions within the studio.

The appointment setter is not the same as a new-business person. Inevitably, new-business people have a whiff of the photocopier sales executive about them: they will be someone who can knock down doors, ring up strangers, and demand to be seen; they will be someone who can conduct presentations that delight CEOs and senior figures in corporations; and they will not be shy, introspective wallflowers. They might even be a shock to our delicate design sensibilities.

Studio heads are often tempted to put salespeople on commission. This is a good idea if we don't care what sort of work we do. But if the type of work we take on is important to us, we should never employ a new-business person on commission. If we pay someone commission, they are going to be very unhappy when they bring us a project and we turn it down because it is not right for us. People on commission often lose the ability to discriminate; they get paid by volume, so they go for volume—and for designers, that's rarely a desirable goal. Instead, a good new-business person needs to be part of the team, sharing the highs and lows of success and failure. They need to be part of a studio's culture. They need to love design and they need to feel that their efforts are as important as those of the designers. They need to know that finding and winning new business is a creative act in itself. By all means, build in a reward or incentive system, but make sure it is the same reward and incentive scheme that exists for other staff. Any other system creates distortions and tensions that are irreconcilable to life in an intelligent design studio.

**How to be a graphic designer, without losing your soul**

If employing an appointment setter or a dedicated new-business person are steps too far, then there's a third option: turn everyone in our studio into new-business people. By encouraging people—especially designers—to think that they also have a business-generating role, and by encouraging people to realize that every gesture, every action, has a new-business consequence, we can go a long way toward finding the work we need. It starts with the junior designers and runs all the way through to the directors. This might sound as if I'm advocating a company of pushy business-fixated automatons. Not so. What it means is that the best people to sell design are designers.

Don't forget that even suppliers and professional advisers can be harnessed into performing an unwitting new-business role; treat them right and they become powerful advocates of our skills. Some of the best work I've ever had has come from being recommended by printers—even my accountant recommended me for a job that kept a team of designers busy for nine months.

### Promotional tools

Regardless of how we win new commissions, we need promotional tools. Even those wonderful clients who call up out of the blue offering us work usually ask if we can "send them something." For casual enquiries it is essential that we have material we can send immediately, or a web site we can direct people to.

The primary tools of communication and promotion for a studio (or a freelance designer) are: its identity (as it appears on stationery or the web site); a portfolio; a web site; and printed literature (which typically might include mailers, flyers, posters, and postcards). There is also the increasingly important area of "extra-curricular activity." By this I mean doing things like curating exhibitions, undertaking research, publishing books or web sites, or indulging in any activity that does not promote ourselves directly. This is before we even get to the most effective and potent tool at our disposal: word of mouth.

### The portfolio

I've already discussed portfolios in relation to designers seeking employment, but creating a studio portfolio to show to potential clients is a different kettle of wriggling eels. When a job-hunting designer shows a portfolio to a prospective employer (usually another designer), they are demonstrating their understanding of design. A subtly different criterion applies when a studio is showing a portfolio of its work to a prospective client; the studio is demonstrating its understanding of communication and the needs of potential clients.

I never once opened up my portfolio in front of a client without feeling a sharp sense of its inadequacy. Of course, if the presentation goes well, then I look at the portfolio as if it were one of Leonardo da Vinci's sketchbooks. This warm glow lasts only until the next presentation, and then the old black doubts return. You would think that a sense of disappointment is a dangerous sensation to experience, yet it is what carries me through presentations. It always forces me to make an adrenalin-charged presentation, and when the day comes that I'm able to open up my portfolio with total confidence and not a shred of self-doubt, I'll know that I've stopped caring and stopped wanting to improve.

Portfolios are emotive things. Designers are never happy with them. I've known many talented designers begin portfolio sessions with an apology: "I'm just about to redo it," they say; or, "Sorry, it's a bit out of date." It seems to be a designer kink that portfolios are "never finished," and never "representative of current work." Although it's not a good idea to start a presentation with an apology, objectivity about our work is hard to achieve; consequently, we are not very good at putting our own portfolios together. This is why we should always ask someone to look at our portfolio and give us a warts-and-all appraisal. It's always faintly shocking to find out what people (especially non-designers) think about our work.

Today we can have a portfolio on a laptop, a DVD, an iPhone—even the well-established if unimaginative black slimline zipper case is permissible as long as it's clean and doesn't look as if it's been slept on. Personally, I find a data projector hooked up to a laptop to be the most effective way to show work. The image is projected onto a wall (it has to be a white wall) and everyone faces the screen. This is great for anyone who is uncomfortable facing a roomful of people; standing at the back of the room as the audience faces the screen is a less challenging alternative. If the work is arranged around a menu, it becomes possible to select work according to the needs of the audience. With a traditional "paper" portfolio, it is rarely possible to accommodate all our work, and I've never made a presentation where I haven't regretted the absence of a particular piece of work: with a laptop and a data projector we can take everything, including screen-based and moving-image work. We can also, of course, take physical samples of work—books, documents, or flyers.

Regardless of how we show our work, we must always try to show it in context. The narrative history of our work and, above all, the results of our work, are what clients most want to see. They don't want to see a succession of arresting images: they want to know what each job achieved.

As designers we are tempted to float our beautiful logo in a sea of empty white space: a little island of graphic cool. Big mistake. This denies our work its narrative power; by far the best way to display work is to show it (where appropriate) in situ. For example, if we have designed a logo that was used by an advertising agency on billboards or in television commercials, show an image of the billboard or a frame from the commercial. We will probably dislike the way the advertising agency has designed the billboard, and the TV commercial might be cheesy, but our client almost certainly won't share our squeamishness.

It's not enough to merely show our work as it was when we were looking for a job as a designer; now we need to show our work *working* and talk about its effects, impacts, and results. This is the secret of a good portfolio.

## Designers' web sites

Most design company web sites fall into two traps; they are either self-obsessed to an unhealthy degree, or they are designed with other designers in mind rather than potential clients. Why is this? Perhaps it's because designers never quite believe that clients hire designers on the strength of a visit to a web site. They are probably right: it's certainly doubtful if many clients trawl the Internet looking for suitable designers to hire; much more likely that they visit a designer's web site only after it has been recommended to them, or if they have been directed there by the designer's own promotional efforts.

**How to be a graphic designer, without losing your soul**

I once did some research into what clients want from a designer's web site. My findings boiled down to one thing: a client list. Only after this need has been satisfied did the prospective clients feel inclined to start digging deeper. It's clear from this admittedly unscientific sampling that most clients want reassurance and endorsement before deciding to make contact with a designer. It seems unlikely that they will be swayed by knowing about the creative director's stag weekend in Riga, or about the piece of work that has just been featured in *1000 Business Cards*.

Any studio that wants to use its web site as a public diary, or as a way of telling other designers what books to find their work in, is perfectly free to do so. But neither approach is likely to win new clients. If, on the other hand, we want to build a web site that will attract commissioners, then our studio web site should be focused on someone who doesn't know us from Adam, and who is not a design obsessive who hangs about the graphic design section of bookstores or loiters on design blogs.

None of this means that web sites should be devoid of personality or that they can't be quirky or unusual. But the web sites that work offer a staging post on a short journey that ends with a face-to-face meeting between client and designer. A web site is like a dazzling multimedia business card. It should excite interest rather than acting like a wet overcoat on a sprinter; it should exude freshness and objectivity, and should avoid self-obsession and info overload. Designers' web sites should be models of clarity and precision; they should say who we are, what we do, who we work for, and how to get in touch with us. Anything else needs careful consideration and a sure-footed approach to talking to strangers who we would like to persuade to buy our professional services.

Promotional literature

I was once part of a design jury that looked at the brochures of various design groups. The results were uniformly depressing. Even the mildly controversial ones ("branding is dead;" "this is not a sales brochure") were formulaic and spirit-sapping. This made me think how depressing it must be to be a client and to be deluged with design company literature. Over the years, I've produced my fair share of this stuff ("…we are a multidisciplinary design group with an innovative approach to…"). My only defense is that I didn't enter any of it into design competitions: I knew it was rubbish. And I knew this because I never got a single piece of work from any promotional literature I ever produced.

What do we do to avoid looking and sounding like everyone else? How do we find a fresh arrangement of words and images that inspires rather than deflates the reader? Even when we produce sharp and distinctive literature, the effect is rarely instant. We've all heard stories about clients who received something in the post from a design company and rang up immediately with an offer of work. It happens, but it's rare. What mostly happens is that clients receive printed matter from designers and then shove them in an ever-thickening file and forget about them or, worse, simply throw them away.

But sometimes, just sometimes, after receiving two or three striking items by mail, and after receiving a friendly call from the designer to ask if the material is of interest, a client might invite us to attend a meeting or join a pitch list. Eureka. We can't ask for much more than this, and as with our web sites, and all our promotional activity, our aim should be to get meetings. The content and tone of any printed literature should be geared to persuading a potential client to see us.

As well as something to send to potential clients, printed literature also serves as an object to leave behind after meetings with potential clients. In the age of the Internet, there isn't much need for expensive brochures. Postcards might be all that's needed, or a flyer, or a cleverly folded leaflet—or even a PDF e-mailed after the meeting. But whatever is decided, we should avoid the visual and linguistic clichés that designers think are essential (they are not; they only serve to make us sound like everyone else). If we don't make fresh and arresting statements in our promotional literature, then, like the pizza flyers we get through our letterboxes, our efforts will end up in the trash.

### Building a reputation

Designers depend almost entirely on their reputations for their livelihoods. Therefore it pays to have a good one. Yet despite the ease with which some people acquire one, a reputation isn't easily gained; it has to be earned, and it has to be forged out of the raw materials of our personalities and our work. Today, such is the appetite for graphic design that many designers—and not just the famous ones—have the spotlight thrown upon them. Even new studios can attain minor celebrity status. Nothing wrong with this, you might think, except that young designers look on admiringly and think, "it must be good to be the object of so much adoration," when in fact too much attention can be destructive.

Being the "next big thing" is rarely desirable. It will perhaps help propel the studio forward for a few months by opening the occasional door and attracting one or two new clients. It will certainly be fleetingly enjoyable to have your views sought by design journalists, and to have work featured in magazines and sexy new design books. But flip back through the design press from the past three or four years, and you'll find designers tipped for success that no one has heard of since; you'll find reviews of monographs from studios that don't exist any more. The reason for this is simple: for every client who is excited by a designer's fame, a dozen others are put off by it. There is even a theory that predicts that if you have too much fame it boils over and scalds your feet.

In a reader's poll run by the British journal *Creative Review*, the eminent British designer Peter Saville failed to be voted "Best Graphic Designer Working Today," a category he'd won on two previous occasions. This was unexpected: the designer had just enjoyed a year of staggering success. He'd held a much-admired one-man show at London's Design Museum; he'd published a long-awaited monograph, and he'd enjoyed an unprecedented (for a designer) amount of coverage from the non-design press.[6]

Patrick Burgoyne, the editor of *Creative Review*, reflected on this: "Peter Saville in particular seems to have suffered from the exposure afforded by last year's Design Museum exhibition and book: from winning best graphic designer two years in a row he now fails to make the top three. It's no reflection on his work or his long-term place in the design firmament, I'm sure, but perhaps an example of the contrary nature of whatever passes for fame in the graphics micro-world."[7]

6   The book was Emily King (ed.), *Designed by Peter Saville*, Frieze Books, 2003. The exhibition was "The Peter Saville Show," held at the Design Museum, London, in 2003.

7   *Creative Review*, October 2004. The designer Mark Farrow won, with Michael C. Place and Stefan Sagmeister as runners-up.

**How to be a graphic designer, without losing your soul**

"Micro-world" is right. Fame in graphic design circles is a bit like fame in dentistry; it doesn't travel beyond the profession. No taxi driver ever heard of any graphic designer. Ever. And for those designers who fancy themselves as iconic figures, there is always the sharp-bladed cynicism of other designers (evidenced in the comments section of any design blog) to act as a sort of quality control filter: we can't fake good work—we really have to do it. Attempts to fake or hype success are always spotted.

### Work done for the portfolio, not the bank balance

When I was building up a portfolio in the early days of running a studio, I sometimes did imaginary work to fatten it up. Not once did any of these phantom projects elicit any interest. Clients could tell they were sham. Self-initiated projects are often essential for an individual's—or a studio's—psychic health. The urge to experiment and explore is perfectly reasonable, and any designer who wants to do personal work should do so. But it is a mistake to think that self-initiated projects will necessarily turn into the sort of work that will attract clients. The blunt truth is that clients are fixated with results; any piece of work without a quantifiable outcome is unlikely to attract the attention of paying customers, even if it reeks of creative excellence.

A much surer way of attracting paying customers is to find a client who will let us do some boundary-defying work in exchange for a substantially reduced fee. This might be work undertaken for a good cause: a charity or a not-for-profit organization. Or it could be an opportunity to give our skills to a client who, in the normal course of events, might find hiring professional designers too expensive. There is an unwritten rule that states: the more money a client spends, the less freedom they permit. But if we find a real living and breathing client who will encourage us to produce groundbreaking work, it will be much more beneficial to our reputations than a self-initiated project.

The design group Browns, founded by designer Jonathan Ellery, has published its own books. The group's output to date adds up to a substantial achievement and has contributed significantly to building Browns' reputation as one of the UK's most accomplished and craft-based design studios. But Ellery didn't set out to produce books that would act as promo-trailers for his company. "On reflection, our early book projects were in response to what we felt at the time to be a very corporate, clinical, graphic design world," he told me in a conversation. "The incentive and the energy to produce our own books came from a mixture of desperation, no clients, and a love of the printed page. I wish I could say there was a commercial or PR strategy in place, but there wasn't. At the time, our accountant told us that it was pointless and to this day still struggles with the concept."

Browns' accountant should wise up. The strategy has paid off handsomely. Today, Browns work for a diverse range of clients, and although their success is down to more than just the books they produce, their small catalogue of lovingly crafted publications has made a substantial contribution to the studio's growth and reputation. As Ellery explains: "People have always found our books of interest, which is very gratifying. They seem to find their way into design, photography, and art magazines, which has given us a profile over the years, and in a way has defined us as a studio. We do a lot of other things, but the books seem to be the projects with the most resonance. It continually surprises me when I get a call from the likes of fashion designer Dries Van Noten asking us to design a book for him. Over the years he had acquired some of our publishing projects and related to them."

Ellery's reluctance to formalize Browns' publishing activities into a calculated promotional activity paradoxically makes them all the more effective as promotional tools. The books are done from conviction—from love, you might say—which makes their impact even more potent. "We're now enjoying a time," Ellery notes, "where the books we have designed and published are strangely creating business opportunities. Image library Photonica is another example of a client paying good money for us to design a book for them. In a funny sort of way our publishing activities—a purely cultural gesture on our part—has made good business sense."

## Design competitions

Opinion is split on design competitions. For many designers, the notion of "competing" like athletes in a race is anathema. You can see their point: winning a design award doesn't necessarily mean that you are "the best." For a start, if we don't enter, we can't win. Plus, we usually have to pay to enter, so only those who can afford the entry fees can take part. This means that if we win a design award, we are only winning "The Best of What's Been Entered" award. Furthermore, we have to submit our work to the scrutiny of fellow designers who are, typically, our rivals. How can we be sure of their impartiality?

Some designers make a point of entering every competition possible on the reasonable premise that if they win they are gifted an invaluable promotional opportunity. (Winners also acquire drab-looking "statuettes" or faux parchment scrolls decorated with bad calligraphy to display in their studios. Which prompts the question: why do design awards usually look so dreadful?) Despite all the moaning and controversy that surrounds the winning entries ("Why did they choose that? I did something identical six years ago"), it usually is the good stuff that wins. Something else I've noticed: I've sat on quite a few design juries, and I'm always impressed by how generous designers are about each other's work. Sure, you meet some sour and resentful individuals, but they are the exception rather than the norm. The first time I sat on a jury I expected it to be a snakepit of fear and loathing, but my fellow jurors were generous, considerate, and tirelessly fair. This has been true of most of the juries I've sat on (not that this precludes some absurd decisions from time to time).

All scruples about design competitions, their artificiality, their fundamental unfairness, vanish when we win. It is very sweet to win a design prize, and winners must publicize and exploit their successes. Send a short e-mail to your clients announcing your win and never forget to include your client in any celebrations—you wouldn't have won it without them.

## Professional organizations

There are numerous professional bodies offering support, advice, and education for fledgling and established designers. Most require membership fees and in return give advice and provide opportunities to learn more about design and design-related matters from fellow professionals. Many designers relish the camaraderie that comes with banding together with like-minded individuals and become energetic participants, often devoting time to sitting on advisory and administration boards at both local and national level. Of course, some designers prefer to remain aloof from communal activities. They see joining design institutions as a step toward losing their independent status and becoming linked to the design establishment, and tend to dismiss professional organizations as smug and self-admiring.

**How to be a graphic designer, without losing your soul**

The fundamental altruism of the various professional bodies and associations, and the degree to which they promote the interests of design and designers cannot be questioned. In recent years, they have made conspicuous and vigorous efforts to become more inclusive, with particular emphasis on helping students and recent graduates. They run lectures and educational sessions and have made extensive and effective use of online material. Inevitably, in their attempt to become all-encompassing, they tend to represent the mainstream: if your interests are in the margins and slipstreams of design and contemporary culture, they are perhaps less relevant to you. Whether you join is a matter of personal judgement.

The question of the ethical position of professional bodies is an increasingly hot topic. For too long, the various national and international bodies have been concerned mainly with tub-thumping on behalf of design and promoting its efficacy to big business. This will need to change as the necessity for an ethical dimension to design activity grows. Voluntary codes of conduct, which were once anathema to designers who relished their free-market independence, are now seen by many as desirable and necessary. In the light of the financial crisis of 2008, society has come to regard ethical conduct as an essential part of the new business and cultural landscape. Anyone who doubts this should visit a few design schools and see what sort of projects the students are choosing to work on; a significant number are electing to work on projects with a social, ethical, or green aspect.

Attending conferences and lectures

There is no shortage of design conferences for the design enthusiast to attend. They are held all over the world in attractive cities that no one minds very much having to visit. They provide congenial opportunities to hear other points of view and to discuss pressing issues with fellow designers. But are design conferences—usually held in the sorts of venues and conference centers that make living in a tent on the edge of a busy road seem attractive—any good?

They are certainly not cheap, yet large numbers of people flock to hear famous designers talk and show off their work. The writer and conference organizer Alice Twemlow wrote an article in *Eye* magazine about the design conference phenomenon: "Design conferences are the places where we hear designers' voices most literally," she wrote. "Yet, of all the apparatus and artefacts that the graphic design community uses as professional buoys, conferences are the least evolved and most perplexing. Books, annuals, magazines and exhibitions are, after all, native territory to graphic designers, and academic curricula and professional associations are firmly established in the discipline's psyche. Conferences, however, are relatively new additions to the field and they sit somewhat uneasily within it. Their styrofoam coffee cups, skirted buffet tables, 'Hello my name is…' badges and PowerPoint presentations bring with them the foreign whiff of Shriners' conventions and the annual industry gatherings of travel agents, car insurance brokers or dentists."

Twemlow is spot-on with her "styrofoam coffee cups" and "skirted buffet tables;" and her comments about the sometimes uneasy fit between designers and the conference arena are shrewd. Having attended conferences both as a participant and as a visitor, I've always learned something—even if it's only to be thoroughly prepared if you're a speaker, and to take some Alka-Seltzer along if you're planning any late-night socializing.

Not as grandiose as conferences, lectures are an essential part of the education of a designer—especially if the lecturer is a good speaker with an interesting tale to tell. I've often been forced to re-evaluate a designer's work after attending his or her lecture. There's something about the elemental format of the lecture room that enables us to get to the heart of the matter.

### Relationships with design schools

There are many good reasons why it's worth maintaining connections with former schools and colleges, or forging links with new ones. Designers have an unwritten duty to pass on their experience and give support to the next generation of designers. It is relatively easy to do this. Colleges are keen to have visits and lectures from professionals. Many designers develop a taste for teaching and discover an aptitude for mentoring. Some become part-time instructors or external examiners, while others enjoy giving occasional talks and presentations. But maintaining links with schools and colleges needn't be just about altruism. Designers have much to gain in practical terms from associations with educational establishments.

In an interview I conducted with American designer Paula Scher of Pentagram for *Design Week*, she identified one of the fringe benefits of teaching: "…It's very good for recruiting. I get to hire the best students," she stated, before going on to say, "…teaching is a great way to have the sort of dialogue I can't have with my clients: about aesthetics, about color theory, about design theory. It's very beneficial to have this other perspective."

I'd add another benefit: today's students are, in some cases, tomorrow's clients. I was once contacted by a woman who ran a large UK government department. She was looking for a design company to undertake a project that would normally be handled in-house by her team of designers. They rarely, she explained, commissioned external studios, but on this occasion the project was too big for her team. To find a suitable design company she had asked one of her designers to recommend a few likely candidates. By chance, the designer she consulted had attended a talk I had given at his school. He'd been impressed and put forward my name. The woman visited our studio, and after the usual formalities, the project was ours.

That was one lecture that paid off. Of course, this is not going to happen every time we give a talk or show some work at a design school. We should view contact with colleges as an opportunity to give something to the next generation, with the confidence that our altruism might be rewarded at some time in the future.

### Dealing with the design press

Exposure in the design press is an important step on the way to acquiring a reputation in the design world. Exposure is desirable and worthwhile, but its effects are cumulative. People need to see two or three pieces of work, or read a few articles or news items, before the word-of-mouth process starts in earnest. When we get our opportunities to bask in the spotlight, we have to be sure that we don't use the moment to make fools of ourselves.

The process of getting work published has been made much simpler by the move away from printed magazines to online journals and blogs. On some sites it is possible to post work directly, but editors and journalists are always on the lookout for fresh voices and new faces, and if we are any good they will find us. Of course, there are ways to help them find us. Develop the habit of sending magazines details of your latest work. Include a brief description of the project in question, the name of the client, and any other relevant information. Keep it brief: if an editor is interested, someone will get in touch. The document, with accompanying visuals, must be sent before the subject is due to be exposed to the public or its intended audience, and it should be sent in plenty of time for the magazine's deadline. Most magazines want striking work, they want newness, they want high-quality images, but most of all they want exclusivity.

**How to be a graphic designer, without losing your soul**

We need to study the design press and decide which magazines and periodicals (online and print) our work is most suited to. It can sometimes be beneficial to appear in a less obvious magazine from time to time, although it can be hard to persuade editors who don't regularly feature graphic design to report graphic design stories. A call to the magazine will determine the publication's deadlines, its policy on receiving submissions, and who to send work to. Look out for special features such as regional surveys or analysis of specialist sectors such as digital design or moving image. Timing is vital: miss an issue and it might mean a wait before work can be included, by which time the project might be old news.

We must also keep in mind questions of confidentiality: does our client want their product exposed before it is launched? Most clients enjoy seeing the work they commissioned written about in a magazine, but it is essential to get their permission. However, the most important thing to remember is that journalists are inundated with material, and there is no shortage of good projects for them to feature. Consequently, they will only use a tiny percentage of what they are sent, so we should only send our best work. Also, I've always made a point of sending material to only one publication at a time. All magazines demand exclusives, so we will quickly run out of friends if we are seen to be flogging our wares to everyone. Choose which magazine is best suited to a project, and send information to them, and them alone.

If you are really hot stuff, you might be made the subject of a profile. Unless you are very confident, I'd avoid giving interviews over the telephone. Sometimes comments and observations are reported wrongly, with dire consequences. One of the first magazine interviews I did was conducted by telephone. The result was a disaster. A busy journalist spoke to me about some work I'd done. In his rush he confused my client with a rival company, and after my client saw it, I spent weeks patching up the rift between him and me. Try and do interviews via e-mail. This gives you time to think about your answer and avoid gaffs. Some journalists prefer to do interviews face-to-face, and you have no choice in the matter: take it slowly, and don't be shy about supplementing your answers via e-mail after the interview.

Designers need regular injections of exposure, but don't let it become a fixation. The benefits are fleeting and transitory at best. Think about acquiring a lasting reputation for good work done consistently over a number of years, not over the past fortnight. If you want to be famous, the first thing you have to do is stop wanting to be famous.

Why there is no such thing as a bad client, only bad client handling. Or why we always blame our clients for our own failings.

**How to be a graphic designer, without losing your soul**

There are no bad clients, only clients turned into bad clients by bad designers. This is a slight exaggeration, perhaps, but only slight. Clients are a bit like dogs: if we feed dogs and look after their basic needs they reward us with loyalty and devotion; but if we beat them and starve them, they become snarling mutts who'd sooner bite your hand than lick it. Same goes for clients: if we want ethical clients we have to be ethical designers; if we want visionary clients we have to be visionary designers; if we want "good" clients we have to be "ultra-good" designers.

   In earlier chapters we've looked at what makes a good designer—but what makes a good client? Well, good clients are rarely compliant; they are usually demanding, inquisitive, infuriating, and maddeningly inconsistent—but with a fundamental sense of fairness. One thing's for sure: clients don't need to "know about design" to be good clients. Some of the best clients I've ever worked with had no previous experience of commissioning design. This contradicts the arrogant, often-heard designer dictum that states "we must educate our clients about design." This is wrong—we must educate ourselves about our clients.

   The poor old client is often masked out of design history and design journalism, not to mention critical and theoretical discourse. If clients are mentioned, it is usually as an amorphous, barely tolerated, and reactionary force, and it is rare for them to be publicly congratulated for their sponsorship, patronage, or encouragement of good design. This chapter speaks up for the clients. Even the ones that bite.


**Dealing with clients**

The writer Robin Kinross, writing about Dutch designer Karel Martens in *Eye*, turned his nose up at the word "client." He wrote: "opdrachtgevers [commission giver], the Dutch word is better than our sleazy 'client.'" You know what Kinross means—there is something sleazy and out of date about the notion of the all-powerful client. But we must resist demonizing our "commission givers;" it's counterproductive. I suggest we try to think of clients as partners: the traditional notion of the client as an all-powerful bestower of commissions is as off-target as the idea of the designer as a humble recipient of the crumbs from the rich man's table. This old model no longer works.

   So how should we deal with clients? Should we treat them like we treat our friends and the people we meet in our social lives, or should we veer toward the more formal protocols of business etiquette? Well, no two clients are the same. They all need something different: this one needs deference; this one is obsessed with value for money; this one is suspicious of designers and unconvinced by arguments about the value of good design; this one is a frustrated designer and wants to be involved in every decision; this one is an enlightened and vigorous supporter of design and designers. The fact that no two clients are the same means that designers have to be hyper-attentive to the individual needs of individual clients. A one-size-fits-all approach doesn't work—nor, for that matter, does a willingness to be all things to all clients.

The best, and only, way to work effectively with clients is to build a partnership based on equality. The Russian-born designer Misha Black co-founded Design Research Unit, one of the world's first design consultancies; his observations on the role of the client are as relevant today as they were in 1956 when he delivered a paper to the Sixth International Design Conference in Aspen, Colorado, called "The Designer and the Client": "I am not suggesting that the influence of the client is necessarily harmful," he said. "The opposite is often true. When the client and the designer are in sympathy, they can together produce better work than that of which either alone would be capable."[1]

Black's observation goes a long way toward answering a question commonly asked by designers: "How can I stop clients making unnecessary changes to my work?" Well, if work is flawed, ill-conceived, or poorly executed, then it deserves to be changed. But, assuming it is none of these things, then the only way to avoid clients interfering unnecessarily is to establish a proper working relationship at the outset. What I'm talking about here is creating the framework for a mature working partnership where we listen and absorb the client's point of view, and where we conduct ourselves in such a way that our client accepts that we have a point of view that's worth listening to.

Of course, attempts to build a partnership don't always work. Like every other designer, I've encountered my share of arrogant know-it-alls; clients who don't want to listen to any advice whatsoever, and who want to control the design process from start to finish. I once worked with a musician who was hyper-sensitive to the minutiae of sound, and to the ways in which musicians should be treated, rewarded, and respected. Yet when it came to design he revealed himself to have no visual sense whatsoever; he treated design like a headstrong kid treats a pile of Lego bricks—"move that there; now move this here." Dealing with him was difficult, but the onus was on me to shake him out of his view that it was okay to treat design in a way that he would never allow his music—or himself—to be treated.

[1] Taken from the paper "The Designer and the Client," reprinted in *Looking Closer 3: Critical Writings on Graphic Design*, Allworth Press, 1999.

**How to be a graphic designer, without losing your soul**

If a client says to you, "I'd like you to incorporate this logo that someone did for me," you can say, "Okay, it will fit in very well" or you can say "Okay," and then seethe internally at its utter inappropriateness. Or, you can take the logo and say, "I'm happy to try it, but I'd like to show you some alternative ideas I have in mind." Most 2 clients will find this suggestion reasonable and acceptable. If they don't, perhaps you should start to worry. All you've done is try to establish a mature relationship that cuts both ways.

I'm not saying I wanted deference from the muso, or that my work should not have been critiqued by him. But I *am* saying that if we want to change our clients' attitude, it won't happen on its own. We have to work at it, and that work begins at the start of the relationship, not further down the line when we realize that the project is not developing in the way we hoped it might. Of course, it is always possible to win over clients at any time in the design process, but the later we leave it, the more difficult it becomes to tell a client that we don't want to include the illustration her school-age daughter has designed. (This has happened to me.)[2]

Establishing a working relationship isn't about always saying yes to our clients. Clients need to be challenged when they are wrong. This is not easy for a designer with no track record, no bulging portfolio of credentials-rich work. Yet, by not challenging our clients when they are wrong, we are doing them and ourselves a professional disservice. As John Warwicker, one of the founders of Tomato, says: "Tell your clients when they are wrong." Of course, we have to learn to do this properly—and just like telling a friend that they have a fault, we have to do it with a mixture of modesty and conviction. Just think how quick clients are to tell us when we are wrong—the same rules apply in reverse.

But what about the opposite situation—those instances when it is us who are in the wrong? As designers, we are not always right, and we have no monopoly on wisdom —although it is common to find designers who think we do. Nothing flags a designer's second-rate status more clearly than the conviction that he or she is never wrong. When I've been pulled up by clients for conceptual errors or mistakes in execution, I've realized that I've been guilty of arrogance or taking a shortcut. So, while we must be quick to defend our work, we must be equally speedy in admitting when we are wrong. Owning up is a sign of strength rather than weakness.

We also need to resist the temptation to tell clients what they should think about the work we have done for them. Why? What's wrong with telling a client that we've done something great for them? Well, telling a client at the beginning of a presentation, for example, that we've produced a terrific piece of work puts them in a position where they are psychologically motivated to disagree. It is the equivalent of a client telling a designer how to design. We hate it when that happens to us; therefore, we must always allow clients to come to their own conclusions before we tell them what we think.

Lastly, despite the huge rise in professionalism within the graphic design world, particularly in the matter of how designers are hired, the majority of clients choose to work with designers that they get along with. I'd be failing in my duty here if I didn't stress the importance of personality in all this. I'm not talking about the need to be a star performer or the sort of fizzy character who lights up a room when they walk into it. There's a place for that, but some of the best designers I've known have been quiet, contemplative individuals who, despite not having a firecracker personality, exude purposefulness and integrity. In fact, there's a place for every sort of character in design, and no two clients want the same thing anyway. Be yourself: that shall be the whole of the law.

## Understanding clients

I'm always suspicious of designers who blame everything on their clients. What they're doing is blaming their own shortcomings as designers on someone else. I'm often told by new (and not so new) designers that they never get offered interesting jobs. Yet when I look at the projects they've worked on, they seem like interesting projects. In truth, most jobs start off the same—unpromising, restrictive, under-budgeted, and with insufficient time allowed to complete them. Of course, it is true to say that designers occasionally find themselves in impossible situations. But unless we undertake work with the conviction that the eventual outcome of any project is in our hands, then we risk failure. Reluctance to accept this reveals a fundamental misunderstanding of the role of the designer, and will almost certainly produce second-rate and mediocre work.

Another familiar misreading of the way clients work is imagining that "so and so" (here designers usually name a famous designer) has been successful because he or she had an indulgent client. This remark is sometimes true. There are indeed "indulgent" clients who act more like patrons than paying customers. But they are rare. In reality, even the exceptional clients have to be won over and tirelessly cajoled into supporting and commissioning our ideas.

Take Neville Brody's epoch-defining work for the British magazine *The Face*. People look at this work and swoon with envy at Brody's good fortune to find such an indulgent client and such a fabulous vehicle to work on. Yet it was Brody who spotted the opportunity, and it was Brody who approached the editor Nick Logan about doing some layouts for the magazine. He was made to wait nine months before being hired to do a few spreads. Most designers would have given up, but Brody kept pressing Logan until he finally gave him the task of designing the magazine. The results became part of graphic design history. My point here is that Brody earned his success. He fought for it. It wasn't handed to him on a plate.

## Keeping clients

There are clients who we sync with from the outset. These are glowing angels of enlightenment who are sent from heaven, and when we find them it's like winning the lottery—only better. But we encounter these celestial figures about as often as we win the lottery. For the most part, clients are real people with real concerns and it requires a huge investment of time, energy, and brainpower to convince them that we are the designers they should be working with. This is not easy: clients are naturally promiscuous, they are presented with temptations everywhere they look, and are free to switch designers like other people switch cell phones. Yet no matter how hard it is to retain a client, it is always easier than finding a new one. And it's worth remembering that the most difficult job we will ever do for a client is the first job we do for them.

First jobs are vitally important in establishing relationships. They are also fraught with danger: we often become impatient and condemn a client as irredeemably bad when it is merely a case of "first job syndrome." First job syndrome is usually caused by our eagerness to impose our ideas and make our presence felt, and by the nervousness of clients caused by apprehension about the final outcome. This is a dangerous cocktail, and often results in another nasty condition—first-job-last-job-syndrome!

## How to be a graphic designer, without losing your soul

How do we avoid losing a client after only one project? Well, by a lot of old-fashioned handholding. Think of it like this: if you saw a blind person about to cross a busy road, would you bundle them through the traffic and abandon them before you reached the other side? Or would you take them by the arm, apply gentle pressure, talk to them, ask them if you are going too fast or too slow, and when you got to the other side, make sure they knew where they were going next and check to see if they needed more help? If we think of our clients like a blind person crossing the road, it's clear that we need to do a lot of metaphorical handholding. It's clear also that we need to explain every step we take; that we need to involve our clients at all stages of the project; that we need to check and double-check all project details; and that we need to produce a rationale for our work that is comprehensible, accurate, and inspirational.

Repeat business is highly desirable, but we mustn't suppose it will happen automatically. I once had a client who I worked with successfully on a project. Later I heard that he was working with another studio. I gritted my teeth and called him: had I done anything wrong? No, he said, I just thought you weren't interested in doing any more work with me. That taught me a sharp lesson.

In the modern business world, long-term relationships with clients are becoming less common. Contemporary business thinking states that businesses need to keep their suppliers in a constant state of alert by chopping and changing them constantly. There is a brutal marketplace logic to this macho business theory, but it is not necessarily the best way for clients to get the best out of designers, where long-term relationships often lead to a deeper understanding of a client's objectives, and ultimately more focused work. It must be admitted that complacency can sometimes set in when we think we have a client for life. Therefore, vigilance is always necessary; we need to look for signs of complacency or patterns of formulaic behavior in our conduct, and we need to be tough with ourselves. If we are not, our clients will do it for us.

Wherever possible, it is worth devoting time and energy to keeping clients. What does this mean in practice? It means taking an interest in their affairs, and it means showing initiative. It means keeping a line of communication open so that they are able to share their thinking and their plans with us. Regular communication should mean just that, and should not mean pestering. For example, if we hire a new member of staff with a new set of skills, we should tell our other clients about it. If we come across some interesting information relevant to our client, we should let them know about it. In the gaps between big projects, if our client needs us to do smaller jobs, such as design invitations or other small items,[3] we should do these tasks with the same relish that we reserve for the bigger projects, and use it as an invaluable opportunity to keep lines of communication open.

[3] Clients sometimes go quiet because they have run out of budget. Perhaps they are waiting for next year's budget to be allocated. If so, small jobs like invitations can sometimes be done at no charge (or at cost) if we are confident that a client will appreciate this gesture, and return the favor when budgets are available.

What about client entertainment? I've never been a fan of client entertainment as a way of generating new business. It is very 1980s. But at the end of a successful project a client lunch can often be a good way to cement a relationship and provide a platform for discussion about future working arrangements. Inviting clients to our studios and hosting a catered lunch sends out a better signal than taking them to a swish restaurant. And it's usually cheaper.

## Sacking clients

We've talked a great deal about finding, developing, and clinging on to clients; sometimes, though, we have to dump them. This should only ever be a last resort; if we are regularly sacking clients it is clearly we who are in the wrong. But there are clients—admittedly not many—who are exploitative and damaging. There are time-wasters and con artists, and we need to develop a sixth sense to spot them. I've encountered many time-wasters, and one out-and-out con-man. Both breeds are easy to spot. They rarely put anything in writing, they don't let you visit them, and they run away if you ask for references.

Not all the clients deserving of the sack are off-putting. I've had delightful, well-meaning clients, who, despite their good intentions, have been unable to pay their bills. When we discover that a client can't pay us, we should stop working with them immediately; we must put them on hold (no more work) until the matter is settled. I've always found face-to-face meetings the best way to resolve situations where clients can't or won't pay. If it can't be resolved, lawyers might be needed, but only when every other angle has been tested.

The best way to avoid sacking clients is to behave professionally at all times (see p. 94). The smiley client clutching a wonderful brief might be a bigger risk than the hard-nosed corporate wolf who wants blood in return for a job. But if we have to sack a client, we should do it professionally. We have to check carefully that we are not opening ourselves up to legal proceedings. We have to check that we have delivered everything we are obliged to deliver. Do they owe us any money? Are there any other implications? When we are satisfied on all these points, and once we've established that the client is worthless, only then should we wield the ax.

## Monopolized by clients

As we become better at finding new clients, better at looking after them, and better at retaining them, we encounter a new problem: over-reliance on one client. Becoming reliant on a single client who accounts for too big a percentage of our business is a serious problem. We should never allow a single client to dominate our business. We are at our most vulnerable when a client monopolizes us: if they leave, we will be stranded with the problem of replacing them.

How do we avoid this? By making the finding of new clients a never-ending priority. Even when we are at our busiest, a part of our energy should always be directed at finding new clients. In an earlier chapter I noted that it's too late to look for new work when we are out of work. The time to look for new work is when we are busy. Like a football team that has just scored, we are energized and brimful of confidence. When we have no work we are hesitant and infected with self-doubt—not a good emotional backdrop with which to attract new clients.

**How to be a graphic designer, without losing your soul**

Professionalism

I mentioned earlier that professionalism is necessary in all our activities. This is a recurring theme in this book. At first glance it seems at odds with my other message—that the life of a creative designer is one of intellectual inquiry, passionate commitment, and creative integrity (by the way, if you didn't know this was a central theme of this book—you do now!). There's even a widespread view among designers that we are better designers if we are poor at business. This is drivel: the better we are at business, the more likely we are to produce meaningful and effective work, and the more professional we are the more likely our clients are to take us seriously. This doesn't mean we have to become corporate clones spouting management speak.[4] What I'm talking about here is the sort of professionalism that is common sense.

        For example, we should always do a credit check on any new clients. I used to be shy about this, but I soon learned that the only clients who get upset about it are the dubious ones. Good clients have no problem with it and view it as sign of a designer's seriousness. Paperwork is anathema to many designers, but we should insist on purchase orders, contracts if necessary, and confirmation e-mails at every stage. For studios that can afford them, a good project manager will take care of all this. But it's vital that it is done, because without it we are putting our livelihoods at risk, not to mention the way we are viewed by clients—most of whom regard professional conduct as a fundamental requirement of any client/designer relationship. Designers who find themselves struggling to do the sort of work they want to do may find that the cause is as simple as a lack of professionalism.

4   Many designers adopt the language and mannerisms of their corporate clients: personally, I've never done this. Even when I've worked with hardcore corporate people, I've made a point of using plain language, plain logic, and common sense—and I've always felt that most of the people I've encountered in corporate land have appreciated this.

Presenting to clients

Presenting to clients is the main test of a designer's communication skills. It is the moment of truth; the moment when we reveal our souls—or at least it's the moment when we discover if we are going to have some income in the weeks and months ahead. Many designers find it intimidating to stand up before a roomful of people and present their work, and for most of us the first half-dozen or so times we do it, it is indeed nerve-shreddingly daunting. But no one expects designers to be orators: you don't have to be Steve Jobs to be good at presenting your work. It's okay to be nervous and awkward, just so long as the work is properly and logically presented. It's okay to be raw and rough-edged, just make sure your presentation is logical and engaging.

When I first started presenting to clients in formal settings I was nervous and sweaty, but I kept doing it and eventually it became, if not exactly stress-free, then at least much less of an ordeal. Sometimes I even enjoyed making presentations—although this only happened when I was totally and absolutely prepared, and when I believed passionately in what I was presenting. When I was less well prepared and less confident about my materials, I had a few telltale beads of sweat to wipe away. The most important factor in making a good presentation is preparation. If we haven't organized every aspect of our presentation, we shouldn't bother turning up.

I always begin presentations by reiterating the brief. Why? Surely the client knows what the brief is—after all, they wrote it? Yes, *they* know what the brief is, but we often hear clients say that designers never follow briefs. Yet by the simple expediency of repeating the brief we can demonstrate that we have in fact understood it. Far from being a waste of time, this simple gesture has a reassuring and calming effect and helps get a presentation off to a good start. Only when our audience is nodding approvingly should we move on to actually showing the work.

This brings us to the great immutable law of making a design presentation: tell your audience what you are going to show them *before* you show it to them.

That's all there is to it. Try it. It works. Yet most designers do the opposite. We throw down a piece of work—something we might have worked on for weeks—and start talking about it as if our client had been with us every step of the way. Big mistake. Work that is as familiar as our own skin to us, can be shockingly new to the client. While we are babbling on explaining what we've done, the poor client isn't listening. He or she is trying to assimilate what is in front of them.

By announcing what we are about to show, showing it, and then clamming up until the first questions are asked, we can help clients to deal with the new and shocking revelation we've placed in front of them. And remember, it's always shocking—*it's never what they expected.*

Now, I know designers who think this is all flimflam. Show the work, they say, and let the work speak for itself; after all, graphic design is supposed to work without any explanations or justifications. True, except "presentations" are not real life—they are artificial. When viewing new work, clients are racked with doubts and uncertainty. Unless we have good reasons for our actions, and present them in a way that allows clients to absorb them, we will suffer the consequences of their doubt and uncertainty.

One of the most helpful steps we can take in a presentation is to give clients time to formulate a response. Too often we demand an immediate reaction. It is far better to encourage clients to "think about it" before giving a definitive response. We've had weeks, perhaps months, to devise this work, yet we expect our client to make up his or her mind on the spot. This is unrealistic. I've often had a poor reaction to an initial presentation, but after encouraging a period of reflection before coming to a final conclusion, I've ended up with a favorable verdict. It doesn't always work, especially if the client uses this as an opportunity to take the work off and canvass opinions. But it's a tactic worth trying when a presentation is met with a hesitant response.

**How to be a graphic designer, without losing your soul**

Regardless of the psychological strategies, and technical niceties of present-ing, a presentation is always about personality. Work has to be good, thinking has to be faultless, preparation has to be exhaustive, but unless we come across as reasonable, rational, and collaborative human beings, our work will fail. We need to talk clearly and good-humoredly. We need to maintain eye contact with everyone (especially the shy intern sitting in for experience). We need to listen to questions and avoid talking over people or dismissing their apparently "stupid" questions. We need to conduct ourselves like decent human beings, even when clients are being unreasonable.

Sometimes a client will ask an inane question, and the temptation to empty the water pitcher over their head will be almost irresistible. But it's probably a good idea to resist the urge. The reason for the inane questions that even quite smart clients ask is that they are mystified by how designers and studios operate. We think they know, but they rarely do. So it can be surprisingly helpful if we tell clients how we operate and how we've reached the conclusions we have come to. These simple acts of demystification can improve the way clients regard us, improve the working relationship—and reduce the need to tip water over their heads.

One last thought: even when we get an instant response, we rarely get formal acceptance or rejection—especially if we are part of a series of proposals that the client is receiving. Usually we leave a meeting with the words "we'll let you know" ringing in our ears. With this in mind, a presentation should also work when we are no longer there to present it. The client often has to present our proposal to other people, so providing a document summarizing our ideas is wise. But we need to be careful how we brand this document. A client from a large company once told me, rather sourly, that she resented the way manage-ment consultants spread their logos across the documentation they presented to her. She found it aggressive and self-promoting. When I present a document to a client, I always put their logo center stage. A client-first policy is rarely wrong.

What is graphic design today? Changing definitions / social design /design thinking / digital design / branding / ethics in design. How global trends in design and culture are materially affecting the lives of graphic designers. Or why graphic design is no longer just about form, shape, and color.

## How to be a graphic designer, without losing your soul

It used to be simple: graphic designers were artisans without much cultural status who received modest rewards for their labors. Graphic design was a craft practiced by people with an eye for form, shape, color, and the attractive presentation of information and commercial messages. Of course, personal taste and fashion also played a part, although it must be said that many traditionally minded designers rejected these last two elements as superfluous and "unprofessional." It was the designer's job, they said, to be a detached reporter of the client's message without overlaying personal taste or clinging to fashionable stylistic gestures.

This definition of graphic design is as outdated as the image of the 1940s commercial artist working at a drawing board with a sheet of paper, a bottle of ink, and a brush tucked behind the ear (think Norman Rockwell). Today, graphic design has altered radically. It encroaches into numerous other disciplines—architecture, technology, entertainment, fashion, public service. It commingles with activities such as writing, editing, research, art, publishing, and entrepreneurialism. To see how design has changed, you only have to look at the way the use of graphic design in the election campaign of Barack Obama has been subjected to the sort of scrutiny normally reserved only for the speeches of presidential candidates.[1]

Graphic design is no longer an invisible Masonic-like craft. Everyone knows what it is, and anyone (with a computer) can practice it—and that's before we start losing sleep over online logo generators[2] and automatic software-driven image compositors.[3] Just as dozens of traditional professional activities (journalism, criticism, auctioneering, encyclopedia compiling) are now being done by energetic "amateur" interlopers with the software to do it for themselves, so too is graphic design. At a time when anyone can be a graphic designer, designers are being forced to ask themselves two fundamental questions: what is our role in modern culture, and what is graphic design in the age of screen-based communications?

Over the next few pages we will look at some of the new ways of being a designer, and some new trends. These newish aspects of graphic design can sometimes feel hard to relate to everyday life—social design, design thinking—especially when we are struggling to pay our taxes and our bills. But the good news is that when we look at these trends carefully we discover that many of them form part of what we do in everyday life anyway.

1   campaignstops.
    blogs.nytimes.com/
    2008/11/20/
    the-o-in-obama

2   logomaker.com

3   vimeo.com/6496886

### Changing definitions

From the 1980s onward, the definition of graphic design changed more radically than ever before. Design became strategized and professionalized. It became the loyal and trusted friend of business, with the result that the status—and incomes—of designers soared. In the 1990s and beyond, this process led to design being subsumed into branding. Many design studios dropped the words designer from their business cards and started calling themselves "branding consultants."

Within design there had always been a few dissenting voices that questioned the role and function of designers. This view became more widespread in the 1990s, when numerous designers resisted the drift toward becoming a subset of consumerism. Many became radicalized by the growth of theory, by the reawakening of design's ethical role, and by what we might call aesthetic politics (the urge to produce non-conformist styles).

There were other changes, too. Graphic design was transformed by the seismic impact of digital technology, and by the rise of new specialized disciplines—motion graphics, information design, web design, interface design.

Although graphic design is still fundamentally about form, shape, color, and the logical presentation of information, it is no longer exclusively about these things. Design in the modern era has to include ethical, social, and technological dimensions. In addition, "design thinking" has been identified as a key component in the drive to find new ways of running businesses and engaging in entrepreneurial activities.

For graphic designers, this de-emphasis on the traditional visual and aesthetic nature of design poses a problem. Designers are people who instinctively see the world in visual terms. Designers are still mostly trained to consider the harmonious arrangement of visual material as their primary function. As a result, we walk around saying, "that looks nice" or "ugh, look at that piece of crap." In other words, we are hard-wired to have opinions about the appearance of things, and we decide what is "good" and what is "bad" using an internal set of aesthetic codes and opinions.

Yet in recent years, a purely aesthetic approach to graphic design has become discredited. This trend has its origins in the influential book *Design for the Real World* by the writer and designer Victor Papanek. He noted: "One of my first jobs after leaving school was to design a table radio. This was shroud design: the design of external covering of the mechanical and electrical guts. It was my first, and I hope my last, encounter with appearance design, styling, or design 'cosmetics.'"

Papanek believed that the area of aesthetics was only a small part of the designer's responsibility. Yet the "look of things"—the aesthetic benefit of beauty and visual flair—is still a fundamental human concern. You might say this has more to do with fashion, peer group pressure, and the psychological need to conform to tribal conventions. But nevertheless, when we abandon a love of visual excitement, form, and proportion, we become a little bit barbaric. Some of the most materially impoverished societies in some of the most remote and underdeveloped parts of the world have the strongest concern for visual exuberance.

Papanek is correct, however, to question our cultural preoccupation with the surface of things. This superficiality is being challenged by numerous factors such as the need to preserve the environment, the need to share global wealth, and the need for a society where we value all human life and not just those human beings who possess good looks, celebrity, talent, and wealth.

**How to be a graphic designer, without losing your soul**

It seems as if we are at a point where we need a new definition of graphic design: one that does not diminish the importance of appearance and aesthetic integrity but that is sustainable (green-focused), democratic (for everyone, not just moneyed elites), and technological (recognizing the way technology has changed the way we live, work, and play).

## Social design

I've always struggled with what is meant by the term "social design." When it is defined as designers doing pro bono work for good causes or taking on voluntary charitable work, I get it; it's easy to understand. But how do we reconcile doing work for "the public good"–often unpaid or for low fees–with the need to earn a living in modern capitalist societies?

I found the answer by accident when I went to visit a friend who runs a successful design group creating wayfinding systems for big cities around the world. His consultancy was booming and he was increasing his staffing levels at a time when most studios were reducing theirs. Here was the answer to the question "what is social design?" Five years ago all this talent would have been employed in the corporate sector working on projects to boost corporate profits. But now here he was creating work with the same degree of professional rigor that once went into corporate work, for projects with a social purpose promoting the common good.

This was a revelation for me; up until then I hadn't grasped that social design doesn't just have to be do-goodism. It can also be real work in the real world–like creating urban wayfinding systems.

Of course, social design isn't new. It's been around since the early Modernists pioneered the concept of good design for everyone. Up until the arrival of Modernism in the early twentieth century, good design, good craftsmanship, and good architecture were benefits enjoyed only by the rich. But with industrialization and mass production, everyone could enjoy the benefits of well-designed artifacts. In the second half of the twentieth century, however, the notion of design for social benefit–design for the common good–was eclipsed by the notion of design as the lubricant of consumer desire, and for most graphic designers, catering for this desire became the basis of their professional practice.

Today the cultural climate has changed yet again, and the "common good" has suddenly become a concept that nearly everyone understands–even big business. What caused this volte-face? There are numerous reasons, but the partial collapse of the global banking system in 2008 was one of the principle factors in causing a change of direction in the zeitgeist. This revolting debacle resulted in national governments scurrying to rescue dozens of banks with taxpayers' money, which in turn caused a widespread reappraisal of the value of unrestricted capitalism and the merits of promoting indebtedness to pay for luxury goods designed by... *designers*.

Another factor was the continuing rise of the environmental movement. Previously it had been a concern of the few, but gradually it became a near-universal concern. In addition, big business began to espouse the benefits of ethical conduct. Fairtrade-certified candy bars started to appear and corporations routinely boasted about their green credentials. Of course, to many people this smacked of corporate opportunism, yet it at least demonstrated that the common good had entered the cultural bloodstream and was offering a small but growing alternative to the desire for endless wealth and endless consumption.

If designers are to earn a living, pay their bills and taxes, and employ other designers, then the practice of social design has to be based in real social and economic practices and not airy rhetoric produced by government-funded think tanks and well-meaning social theorists. I'm also aware that there is a great deal of holier-than-thou hypocrisy surrounding the question of the "common good." So what does it mean in practice for the average designer?

It means questioning what we do and who we do it for. Easy to say, less easy to do. Except that there is now a genuine shift toward a more ethical and socially responsible position in all walks of life. I admit that this shift is not universal, but you can see it in countless, often unlikely, places. The most surprising institutions are making inroads into the realm of social responsibility.

When designers make concern for social issues as strong as their concern for aesthetic and conceptual integrity, it will no longer be a bolt-on sentiment. It will be a fundamental component in the designer's kit bag of attitudes, beliefs, and practices. Of course, this might be wishful thinking on my part. But somehow I don't think so.

I see a huge interest in design with a social focus in the design schools I visit regularly. It appears to have replaced the dominant concern of students over the past two decades, which was stylistic: students wanted to produce radical design in the way many now want to create design with a social purpose. The style wars have been replaced by the ethical wars. When this generation of designers forms a significant percentage of the population of professional designers, then design will no longer be regarded as nothing more than the sweetly scented lubricant of consumerism.

## Design thinking

The phrase "design thinking" gets bandied about almost as much as "social design." The term has become fashionable in progressive business circles. In a recent *New York Times* article "Welcoming the New, Improving the Old,"[4] the writer Sara Beckman described how business growth in recent decades has been driven by the tools of measurement and analysis. But she goes on to describe how a new dimension to business thinking is being achieved by utilizing the ways in which designers think.

As an example of the effectiveness of design thinking, Beckman cites the example of Jeff Denby and Jason Kibbey. While still at business school, they developed the online underwear company Pact[5] and according to Beckman, they applied design thinking to evaluate how customers use and buy underwear. The duo 'visited underwear stores and asked friends and family to send pictures of the underwear in their dresser drawers, or, for those brave enough, shots of themselves posing in their favorite boxers or panties. They tested different approaches to marketing, including subscription programs, and different ways of developing stylish products. For example, they considered letting up-and-coming designers compete to create designs showcasing particular causes.'

4 businessweek.com/design-thinking

5 wearpact.com

## How to be a graphic designer, without losing your soul

Today, Pact sells organic cotton underwear created by the designer Yves Béhar. The designs use graphics that highlight the work of groups engaged in socially beneficial activities and a portion of revenue is donated to these causes.

Designers will recognize Pact's freewheeling, "what-if" approach. As a business strategy, it seems to *anticipate* new circumstances rather than relying on past trends and patterns. But if this is what is meant by "design thinking," how is it different from any other type of thinking?

6   Taken from Roger Martin, *The Design of Business: Why Design Thinking is the Next Competitive Advantage*, Harvard Business Press, 2009.

In "What is Design Thinking Anyway," a brilliant essay by Roger Martin posted on *Design Observer*,₆ the author defines the two dominant types of logical thinking as deductive reasoning and inductive reasoning. He defines deductive logic as reasoning from the general to the specific. He gives an example: "If the general rule is that all crows are black, and I see a brown bird, I can declare deductively that this bird is not a crow." Inductive logic, on the other hand, reasons from the specific to the general. Martin writes: "If I study sales per square foot across a thousand stores and find a pattern that suggests stores in small towns generate significantly higher sales per square foot than stores in cities, I can inductively declare that small towns are my more valuable market."

The writer notes that these two modes of thought—deductive and inductive—allow the thinker to declare "at the end of the reasoning process that a statement is true or false." He then cites the work of American philosopher Charles Sanders Peirce: "[Peirce] argued that no new idea could be proved deductively or inductively using past data. Moreover, if new ideas were not the product of the two accepted forms of logic, he reasoned, there must be a third fundamental logical mode. New ideas came into being, Peirce posited, by way of 'logical leaps of the mind.' New ideas arose when a thinker observed data (or even a single data point) that didn't fit with the existing model or models. The thinker sought to make sense of the observation by making what Peirce called an 'inference to the best explanation.' The true first step of reasoning, he concluded, was not observation but wondering."

Peirce named this form of reasoning "abductive logic." Many designers will recognize it as a description of what they do in their work. When we use deductive or inductive thinking we come to *therefore* conclusions, but when we use design thinking, we arrive at *what if* conclusions: in other words, we wonder.

"What if" thinking is maddening to many pragmatic and cautious clients. It often leads them to think of designers as stubborn, cussed, and contrary, when in fact, designers are just thinking differently. But you can also see why certain sorts of progressive businesses and social ventures might like this kind of imaginative, non-deductive thinking.

In truth, we need all kinds of thinking to be a designer. As well as being creatures of imagination, we have to live in the world of budgets, schedules, and an ever-changing business and cultural landscape. As Roger Martin points out, "the prescription is not to embrace abduction to the exclusion of deduction and induction, nor is it to bet the farm on loose abductive inferences. Rather, it is to strive for balance."

Digital design

We're all digital now. In many parts of daily life, the digital way is now the norm. Life is unthinkable without our digital life-support systems of smart software and sleek gizmos. When I lose something in my studio—a book, a pen, a page of working drawings—my first thought is to tap the name of the missing item into Google. Then I remember: even Google isn't that smart.

Where does the digitization of life affect the graphic designer? For a start, digital culture has opened up a vast arena of work that didn't previously exist for designers. This is a good thing; any designer with the basic skills that enable him or her to build a simple web site or capture and edit filmed footage will never starve. And yet, in a world where anything converted into a digital file can be zapped across the globe in the time it takes to think about it, what need is there for the graphic designer's traditional skills of visual communication? In a world where an iPhone can connect us instantly to billions of other human beings, what is the point of 1,000 years of typographic tradition? In an age of gestural interactivity, what is the role of color and form? And here's an even bigger question: are graphic designers the best people to be creating the new digital communication products and services of tomorrow?

Paradoxically, digital design takes us back to the description of the traditional graphic designer with which we began this chapter: the faceless servant creating something that works without any personal intrusion whatsoever. Take interface design, for example. Interface design is unlikely to produce superstar designers who are feted and admired for their showy flamboyance. Yet unimaginably vast numbers of human beings are entirely dependent on the way interfaces are designed.

In an article titled "The Digital Challenge: Making Easy-to-use Devices,"[7] the British design critic Alice Rawsthorn wrote about interface design: "Its goal is to ensure that all of us can use digital devices simply and intuitively, regardless of how techno-savvy we are. As we're spending more and more time with digital products, UI [user interface] is becoming one of the most important areas of design, but it's also one of the trickiest to judge. When user interface design is good, it's hassle-free and we don't have to think about it; but when it's bad, it can make our lives hell."

A recent survey into the uptake of the Internet among older and disadvantaged people was recently undertaken by a body funded by the British government.[8] The report got widespread attention when it highlighted the problem many people have with the need to hit the Start button in Microsoft Windows to *close* the software. This anomaly was widely cited as the sort of typical failure of interface design that stopped many people from using computers, and there's no doubting the fact that poorly designed interfaces are a major impediment to the comfortable use of numerous devices.

7   nytimes.com/2007/02/25

8   raceonline2012.org

If we accept the old notion of design as a marriage of form and function, then interface design turns a century of design thinking on its head. Here we have design where function is paramount and form is secondary: if you notice the font or colors used to make the interface of your MP3 player, they are probably wrong. This takes us back to an older notion of what graphic design is, and it reverses the developments of the past few decades where design has become valued for its ability to be admired and relished for its stylistic heft.

**How to be a graphic designer, without losing your soul**

And it's because of this that interface design and digital design in general attracts a different type of graphic designer from the sort we've come to accept in recent decades.

The digital designer is often more like a scientist than an artist, requiring a high degree of intellectual wattage, not to mention an understanding of technology and software. Designers have always required technical know-how, but this was limited to printing techniques, mechanical and electronic typesetting, and image creation (photography, illustration, and printmaking). Today, the digital designer needs a far wider sphere of knowledge. The digital designer is required to work with computer code, hardware specifications, and usability theory.

The consequence of this huge rise in technical and other demands on the modern designer is the increasing necessity for, and dependency on, collaboration. There was a time when designers were able to work solo. But in the high-tech digital domain, this is rarely an option. When we couple this with the single biggest change in graphic design since the arrival of computerized design in the 1980s—design (mainly web pages) that can be controlled, altered, even generated by the user—we see that the digital designer has to be a new sort of practitioner. There is no room for the old control-freak designer who managed every square millimeter of a page with microscopic control and worked in splendid isolation. The digital designer is a new type of designer with a different approach to visual communication and a new collaborative sensibility.

Can anything be learned from the great tradition of graphic design thinking and practice, or should the teaching of typographic pioneers such as Emil Ruder and Jan Tschichold have to be tipped into the dustbin of history? Have these seminal figures been replaced by usability theorists, behaviorists, and brand and marketing wonks as the people designers should be listening to?

Hilary Kenna, a lecturer in Design and Digital Media at IADT in Dun Laoghaire, Ireland, has made a study of the links between typographic pedagogy and the digital realm, and in her view the teachings of Ruder and Tschichold are as relevant today as they were forty to fifty years ago. In an e-mail to me, she wrote: "The fundamental principles of typography are still concerned with communication, aesthetics, and legibility. Ruder's ideas transcend technology, he offers design principles at a critical conceptual level which can be adapted to any media—he presents a way of thinking and making typography that is flexible and open to creativity but underpinned by systematic methods. In an era dominated by style and technology, it is worth revisiting some of his core ideas to find ways of building new approaches for screen."

Kenna sees work in the digital domain that exemplifies the teachings of the Modernist masters: "There are examples of innovative screen typography that may signal future directions for the discipline. The early work of John Maeda, David Small, Yugo Nakamura, or the likes of Spin and Fred Flade are interesting for their experimental yet disciplined approach. They use minimal means to extort maximum expression and the attention to detail in motion and interactivity is so natural it almost goes unnoticed. This type of work demonstrates how modernist approaches to typography remain relevant today. The likes of Emil Ruder, whose ideas transcend technology, provide a solid basis in aesthetic and functional design principles from which to experiment and adapt for new media."

For Kenna, the quality of screen typography is usually determined by the level of technical know-how of the designer or the aesthetic sympathies of the programmer. "This is why web themes and templates have taken such a foothold," she notes. "Because creating detailed screen typography is time consuming and difficult. Interestingly, the emergence of a minimal aesthetic and a focus on grids has unconsciously created a renewed interest in Modernist typography. Much can be learnt from the likes of Emil Ruder and Jan Tschichold, whose design principles offer a solid grounding in aesthetic, functional, and interpretative aspects of typography, irrespective of media."

Usability is undoubtedly the single most important aspect of the design of a web site and nearly all forms of interactive communication. A web site selling rail tickets that is hard to use is as useless as a car with no steering wheel. But how is usability thinking affecting the design and build of web sites? Is good design compatible with usability? As the American web designer Dmitri Siegel notes elsewhere in these pages, it is critical that design and functionality go hand in hand: "For me, it permeates the entire design process. The first step of building a web site is the preparation of requirement documents. That's when you think about yourself and what you (or the client) want, and obviously you want people to be able to use the thing."

So far, so normal. This is how nearly all designers think when they start a new project. Except, as Siegel goes on to say, web-based projects benefit from designers working simultaneously with programmers and usability experts: "The design process begins in earnest with wireframes and screen-flows. This is the lion's share of the design process and it is incredibly creative. The important thing here is that the graphic designer works on the screen-flows, not just a developer or information architect. In many other offices, the designer gets handed a site that is basically engineered rather than designed and these end up being very soulless. You have to have constant interchange and collaboration between designers and developers. They have so much to teach each other. This process naturally flows into the visual design process. If you have strong wireframes it's very liberating for the graphic designers because they know that all the user interaction is covered and they can take more risks with the presentation and interaction aspects."

There are many other sorts of digital design besides the design of web pages. Designers are making installations, digital films, audio sequences, iPhone apps, complex interfaces, and investigating ways of making newspapers and books work on handheld devices.

I recently spoke to a publisher friend who runs a well-established monthly magazine with a global readership. We got to talking about the need for his magazine to have a digital version online. He told me that the PDFs that are sent to the printers are also posted online for subscribers to the publication. But—as he pointed out ruefully—the uptake of the digital version was poor. When we discussed it further we agreed that the version that works in print doesn't work as the digital version. The digital version needs to be redesigned and optimized for online use.

It is for reasons such as this that designers are at the heart of the digital revolution. Without a designer, my friend can't optimize his material for digital use. Which seems to put designers at the center of the digital transformation of communications. I'd go even further and say that the transformation will not happen without designers, and that any designer who possesses the basic digital skills is superbly well equipped to deal with the seismic upheavals that are already taking place within the media universe.

**How to be a graphic designer, without losing your soul**

Branding

The problem with branding—for graphic designers—is that anything works. Any mark, shape, splodge, or typographical concoction will do, just so long as it is deployed with ruthless efficiency and total conviction. This means, however, that the craft of graphic design is not much valued in branding circles. Really anything will do—it doesn't even have to be well designed.

The clear and honest expression of identity is one of the most important aspects of modern commercial life. In a world dominated by the visual, businesses and organizations have to be able to offer a sign, a symbol—a house style—that identifies them. This has been true since the start of the modern age (even earlier if we think about heraldry and tribal insignia), and graphic designers have been very successful at creating these badges of identity.

But identity is no longer enough. Today, organizations need *branding*—or so we are told. Conventional wisdom dictates that everything needs to be a brand: TV shows are brands, candy bars are brands; even nations are brands. In truth, however, they are not brands; they are TV shows, candy bars, and countries. When we persist in thinking of them as brands and not what they really are, we enter a different plane: a plane of unreality and often, it has to be said, of deception. When the primary focus of a TV show is to become a brand, it's almost certainly a second-rate TV show. People buy candy bars for their taste. They may accept and be guided by the brand ethos of the candy bar, but if the chocolate suddenly starts tasting like pepper they will stop buying it. And when countries decide to bring in branding consultants it is usually because they have made a mess of running those countries, and branding isn't going to change the social consequences or the global view of that ineptitude.

This is the problem with branding: it has become more important than the thing it purports to brand. When that happens, unreality and deception become the norm. But what does this mean for the modern graphic designer?

For many, it's good news. The growth of branding has meant that there are many more opportunities to practice design and earn a good living. But in the long run, I'd say that designers' willingness to hook themselves up to the branding war machine that has slashed and burned its way through global business culture in the past decade has resulted in the diminution of graphic design as an autonomous stand-alone discipline. The result of this can be summed up in a single phrase: a loss of faith in the intrinsic value of graphic design.

I say this for three reasons:

1       Branding is a business fad that will decrease in importance in the coming years, and because it has yoked itself to branding, graphic design risks being sucked down with it.
2       The role of design as a stand-alone discipline has been diminished by its junior status within the branding process.
3       As branding is increasingly seen as little more than spin and hype, and part of the coercion industry, design becomes tarnished in the eyes of users and practitioners alike.

Let's look at each of these assertions in detail. Branding as business fad: surely branding is part of the thinking of every business and institution, making it unlikely to be jettisoned anytime soon? Yes, but as branding fails to produce the results it claims to be capable of generating, it will increasingly be subjected to scrutiny from accountants and business analysts. It wouldn't be the first business creed or philosophy to fall out of fashion and become discredited. Our leaders thought it was a good idea in the post-communist era, for example, to deregulate the financial markets. This became a near-universal belief, but who believes in it now? Everywhere there are calls for more intervention and regulation of financial markets.

And look at what happened to Wall Street's Masters of the Universe. Who would have guessed that their financial wizardry would be exposed in 2008 as not much better than banditry, and that they'd have to go begging to the government for a bailout?

In his book *Obsessive Branding Disorder*,[9] the business writer Lucas Conley notes the extent to which corporate America is in thrall to the cult of branding. In Conley's view, this has led to the abandonment of the "trusty, dusty principles of business—innovative products, good service, solid management" in favor of the "idealism of branding...." He berates corporate leaders for becoming "so focused on the strength of the all-encompassing idea —the brand—that they ignore the physical properties that compose it." In other words, branding has become the quick fix that promises instant success: why bother with expensive improvements to products and services when a new logo, a ritzy strapline, and a brand guidelines book can do the job just as well and at a fraction of the cost?

9 Public Affairs, U.S., 2008.

As more and more businesses fail to find salvation in branding, the discipline itself will be called into question. Branding can easily end up in the same bin as sub-prime mortgages and debt transfer schemes—exposed as valueless. In a neat irony, it should be noted that all the banks and institutions that failed or required bailing out with taxpayers' money boasted "good branding."

The second allegation is that design has slipped down the food chain as a result of its envelopment within branding. This seems inarguable. The leading brand thinkers are not designers; they are businesspeople and marketing people. This new breed of brand evangelists fall over themselves to point out that a brand is more—much more—than a mere logo. This is true. Yet in their lust to get the ears of senior boardroom people, the brand evangelists have pushed the messy business of design to the end of the chain of command, thus diminishing designers in the eyes of their clients.

It also means that design within numerous industries is controlled by non-designers; or, to put it another way, marketing and communications people wearing the impenetrable body armor of a thick brand manual. This has led to the eradication of variety, diversity, and interest. It has led to the anodyne nature of modern communications. And it has led to the relegation of design to a minor position within the communication strategies of companies.

Yet perhaps the greatest disservice that brand evangelists do to design—and their clients—is to add mystique and complexity to what is really a simple process: they do this by spouting brand verbiage and using the language of obfuscation. Design has suffered damage from this process—it will struggle to repair this damage.

**How to be a graphic designer, without losing your soul**

Thirdly, I mentioned the ethical question. This is trickier. Not everyone sees branding as unethical—and in truth, most of it isn't. But it has become lumped in with spin, hype, and the black arts of PR; it has become tarnished with the toxic overspill of untruth and manipulated truth. In other words, branding is not always honest—and in some cases, nakedly deceptive.

This is not to say that graphic design has always been pure and unsullied. Someone designs the logos for landmine companies; someone designs cigarette packaging; someone designs the brand identity for oil companies who dump toxic waste in Africa; and as designers we are up to our eyes in "greenwash."[10] So we cannot claim to have a monopoly on virtue. But we can claim to have a tradition of honesty and integrity that we can revive if we choose to remember that graphic design is about the way a company presents itself truthfully and not the way it would like to be seen.

10  A term used to describe the practice of companies disingenuously spinning their products and policies as environmentally friendly.

I realize that my list of reasons for why branding is bad for graphic design puts me into a minority within design. Most designers seem content to absorb themselves into branding. But are they doing anything other than creating a house style?

I rang my insurance company the other day and talked to a robot. It turned out to be a real human being, but he was working to a set of call-center commands that meant he might as well have been an android from the planet Zonk. After a short conversation, I switched my insurance policy. As far as I was concerned, I didn't want to deal with this company. But this is a company with—in professional terms—a good brand identity. I'm sure its brand guardians would talk about the need to offer a "totally on-brand service at all customer touch points." Yet its "customer touch" was about as helpful as a drunk on the subway at midnight.

I mention this to show that a corporation's brand identity is dependent on dozens of factors beyond the control and experience of graphic designers. In truth, it is beyond the control of the advertising and PR wonks who talk the brand talk. There is an important role for designers in the creation of honest, functional, and clear depiction of any venture's public-facing image, but when that becomes confused with the creation of what the brand gurus call brand values, problems ensue.

## Ethics in design

We have already touched on the subject of ethical conduct in the section on Social Design (see p. 100). Ethical conduct has become a growing concern among designers in the past few years.

This concern can also be seen in the wider culture, as people recoil from two decades of rampant greed and exploitation, and turn instead to what the political philosopher Michael Sandel has called "a new citizenship" founded on a "politics of the common good."

But what does this mean for designers earning a living in the modern world? It certainly doesn't mean that we have to stop designing non-essential items such as the labels for shampoo bottles, lottery cards, or bus tickets. As designers, why would we not want to see these things "well-designed"? What I'm suggesting, however, is that we have to design shampoo labels and lottery cards and bus tickets with an ethical dimension.

Really? What have ethics to do with shampoo labels? Well, we could start by looking at the meaning of the word "ethics." There are various definitions of ethics, but the one that is most relevant to us here is:

"The rules of conduct recognized in respect to a particular class of human actions or a particular group, culture, etc.: medical ethics; Christian ethics."[11] To this list of particular groups we could add design ethics, which means that we can say that ethics in design relates to the rules of conduct in respect to being a designer.

11 dictionary.reference.com/browse/ethics

Back to the shampoo, then. The world wouldn't come to an end if shampoo ceased to exist, but it would be a less hygienic place without it. And if it is to be sold in stores, it will need labeling stating the product's name and ingredients.

Yet a shampoo label will work just as well without foil blocking, complex die-cutting, or six special colors—in other words it will work without the wasteful and extravagant use of the world's diminishing resources. That's before we even start to think about the truthfulness of any claims that the manufacturers make about their product. If when we are designing the labels we are asked to say "not tested on animals," we need to be sure that this is true, or we are complicit in a deception.

We need to give the same weight to ethical concerns that we would normally give to stylistic and commercial considerations. At its most basic level, if we want to design ethically in a world of diminishing resources, we have to make an effort to only design stuff that needs to exist.

To many ears, this will sound like smarmy do-goodism. But when we incorporate an ethical dimension into our work as naturally and instinctively as we do with our creative ideas and our ideas about commercial effectiveness, such thoughts will feel less pious and more like common sense. I'm going to stick my neck out here and say that as more and more clients move toward an ethical position, there is a real opportunity for designers to become exemplars of ethically focused activity.

I've always believed that ethics for designers are a matter for individuals to decide for themselves. But I wonder if we've reached a point where we need some help from professional design bodies? We have national laws to prevent wrongdoing, and we have inherited traditions of morality to help us decide what is right and wrong. Yet ethics are a matter for individuals and groups to decide for themselves, and the professional practice of design is free from professional ethics—or at least institutionally enforced ethics.

This is odd—most mature professions have them, and you can be "struck off" for transgressing them. Some of the older professional design bodies have had ethical codes, but they fell out of fashion in the deregulated 1980s and 90s, which coincidentally, was the point when design was at its most expansionist and competitive.

**How to be a graphic designer, without losing your soul**

So have we reached a point where we should all sign up to a professional ethical code? The arguments in favor of an ethical code for designers are compelling. Much energy is expended on fretting and railing against the unfairness and sharp practices of clients and commissioners of graphic design. This could be lessened by the simple act of all designers uniting behind an ethical code that gives guidance on such matters as unpaid spec work or theft of ideas. But I can't see it happening.

One of the reasons for this, of course, is that ethical codes cut both ways. We want them to knock our clients into line, but are we prepared to live with the effects that an ethical code will have on our activities as designers? It is common for designers to demand that they are treated ethically—we say no to spec work; no to unpaid competitive bidding; no to theft of ideas; no to poaching staff; no to unrealistic demands from powerful clients. But how ethically clean are we? What about our conduct toward interns? Do we pay them, and can we be sure that we are not guilty of a bit of old-fashioned exploitation? Do we have any illegal fonts on our hard drives? Have we ever used an image that we shouldn't have used? Have we ever used another designer's work in a "mood board" presentation to one of our clients? Have we loaded a bill to a client? Charged for a service we didn't supply? Charged for time we didn't work?

Perhaps unethical practices—among clients *and* designers—will be eradicated in the way that "bad design" has been eradicated. We may deplore much of the homogenized graphic design and branding that surrounds us, but we can't say it is "bad" in the sense that it is amateurish or poorly rendered. It is invariably technically, conceptually, and cosmetically "good." This didn't use to be the case, and it was common to see yelpingly "bad" design. But as the status and self-belief of designers rose, so did their ability to promote good design, and the bad stuff became less and less prevalent.

My belief—okay, my hope—is that ethical thinking will come to be part of the designer's tool kit in the same way that creative and conceptual thinking is. For many, it always has been. It's just that some of us have some catching up to do.

Analysis of creativity at a time when most graphic design is about sameness and following formulae. Or why creativity means taking risks.

**How to be a graphic designer, without losing your soul**

Creativity is a word that is used a lot; sometimes in a flattering way, sometimes in an unflattering way. To be creative is seen as a good thing; however, "creative accounting" usually means dishonest accounting. Advertising people who make brilliant and original ads, that become part of the cultural life of nations are called "Creatives," but so are the ones who steal ideas from YouTube. Big corporations say they value creativity, yet very few are run by creative people; instead they are run by accountants, lawyers, and pragmatic business-people—non-creative people.

1    Malcolm Gladwell,
*Outliers: The Story of
Success*, Little, Brown
and Company, 2008.

Although creativity is admired, creative people are often seen as unreliable and not quite serious. But as any truly creative person will tell you, the creative process is really about hard work and dedication, with only a tiny part given over to naked inspiration. The pop philosopher Malcolm Gladwell (author of *Blink: The Power of Thinking Without Thinking* and *The Tipping Point: How Little Things Can Make a Big Difference*) noted in a recent book [1] that "composers, basketball players, fiction writers, ice skaters, concert pianists, chess players, master criminals, what have you..." have devoted 10,000 hours to practicing before really achieving success. Although Gladwell's argument relates to success in general rather than creativity, and despite the niggling question—is that *exactly* 10,000 hours or will 9,999 do just as well?—the link between graft and success in any area is real.

So, if there is no inbuilt power-on switch for creativity, how do we ensure that a steady current of ideas and inspiration will flow through our brains? In this chapter we will look at some of the factors that drive creativity in designers.

**What is creativity?**

Creativity is about risk-taking, it's about the rejection of comfort, and it's about sweat—not the sweat of fear but the sweat of hard work. I'll allow that there is a place for sudden inspiration, too—but inspiration only occurs when risk, discomfort, and graft are also involved. Here's my creativity equation:

risk + discomfort + sweat ($\pm$inspiration) $=$ creativity.

Let's do the math, as people say. I once read that to ensure good mental hygiene, homo sapiens have to flirt with death at least once a day. This doesn't mean entering war zones or climbing sheer rock faces, but it might mean being narrowly missed by a speeding car as we cross a busy road, or walking under scaffolding as giant blocks of concrete are swung over our heads. It's the same with any creative endeavor: we have to flirt with failure if we are to produce anything with the sap of genius in it. If we don't occasionally look into the abyss, we end up producing work that has all the excitement of a pair of well-worn carpet slippers. To put it bluntly, there is no creativity without risk.

We avoid risks because we wish to avoid failure. But by embracing failure as a necessary and welcome step on the way to achieving meaningful creative work we will find that our creative output is richer and less predictable. The writer and semiotician Umberto Eco noted that modern science "is based on the principle of 'fallibilism' … according to which science progresses by continually correcting itself, falsifying its hypotheses by trial and error, admitting its own mistakes—and by considering that an experiment that doesn't work out is not a failure but is worth as much as a successful one because it proves that a certain line of research was mistaken and it is necessary either to change direction or even to start over from scratch." Fallibilism should be the guiding principle for all graphic designers.

We can be sure, however, that there is no such thing as effortless creation, even if it often seems as if talented people live in a frictionless world where nothing holds up their creative flow. Ideas that arrive quickly and without mental turmoil are often seductive and engaging, but when examined after the sugar rush of inspiration has passed, they turn out not to be as good as we first thought, or are found to be in need of the added nutrients that come from more brainwork. This is especially so in the digital domain, where fallibilism becomes doubly relevant. The computer, with its speed-of-thought processing power, enables the designer to explore and execute ideas with a twist of the wrist. But there is no advantage in this ability to experiment if we don't use it as an opportunity to risk failure: the high-wire acts we admire most are the ones that do it without a safety net.

Back to the equation: there is no creativity without discomfort. I've often wondered why so many great artists, designers, musicians, and writers reach a point where they cease to produce new and fresh work. It is common for talented individuals who have made groundbreaking statements of dazzling originality, to suddenly start repeating themselves. They often do this brilliantly yet without the fire-truck rush of pure invention that characterized their earlier work.

For most creative people, a point is reached where they become so confident in their own abilities that their work becomes repetitive and predictable. They become comfortable. And we don't have to be seventy years old to reach this point, either. Comfort can set in at any time. But to be a creative person is never to be comfortable: the creative condition is a near-permanent state of self-scrutiny, self-discovery, and self-doubt. The moment we think—*hey, I'm good*, is the moment we get hit by the ricocheting bullet of ordinariness. Ouch.

The third part of the creativity equation is the sweat part, or to put it another way—hard graft. Graphic designers don't sweat—well, not when wrestling with design tasks. But we need mental stamina, which can be almost as draining as the stamina we need to run a marathon or climb a mountain. Maybe "energy" is a better word than sweat? I'm thinking about those times in a project when we say to ourselves—*that'll do*. But what if by expending just another ounce of energy we get to another point further on—or reach a point where we are able to fully evaluate an earlier idea and recognize its worth and value? Well, we only reach these points by expending energy—by working up a sweat.

The final part of my equation—*plus or minus inspiration*—is not an attempt to downgrade or inflate the importance of inspiration, which is usually seen as something external or god-given, or something that has nothing to do with the individual concerned. People talk about *waiting for inspiration* as if it were a train or a bus that they have no control over. The idea that inspiration comes from an external source—divine or natural—is unhelpful. Inspiration comes from within, and if we rely on it to turn up like the breath of God, or without the other parts of the creativity equation, we will be disappointed. And yet *inspiration exists*, and when it hits, its appearance is always somewhat miraculous; this is why I say that we can *add or subtract* inspiration to the creativity process, but we can't rely on it alone; it has to be bundled up with risk, discomfort, and sweat.

**How to be a graphic designer, without losing your soul**

The brief

I was talking to the members of a small design group recently. They were ambitious, talented, and articulate, yet they complained that they weren't progressing as well or as fast as they would like to. We talked about the possible reasons for this, and then one of them said, "of course, we rarely get proper briefs from our clients." This snippet of information provided one of the main reasons why the group was not progressing.

All design jobs should start with a brief; designers need briefs like newsreaders need news. If designers didn't need briefs they would be artists or Polar icecap explorers– anything, in fact, except graphic designers.

Briefs can be verbal or written. Sometimes briefs can be a discussion. That's okay, too. But it always pays to get clients to put briefs in writing: it adds clarity and it forces a thorough examination of the subject. I have clients–usually long-standing ones–who send me a photograph and a few words of text, and say: "Poster by Friday, please." They know that I know what they want, so nothing more needs to be said. Nevertheless, the first duty of a graphic designer is to demand and receive a proper brief.

But what is a *proper brief*? And what happens if we don't get one? Well, the second question is easier to answer than the first. If we don't get a brief we should demand one, and if we still don't get one we should either write our own or dump the client. I don't say that lightly–dumping clients is a serious business and should only be contemplated when all other approaches have failed. But a client without a brief is a bad client. They can never be satisfied (They say: "I'm not sure about this"), and they can never be wrong (They say: "This is not what I wanted"). So, no brief–no client. Yet long before we get round to sacking a client who refuses to give us a brief, we should try writing our own. This tactic will only work, however, if we then show it to our client and get them to agree to it. It also has the advantage of preventing us from being accused of "ignoring the brief"–an accusation frequently leveled at designers.

But back to the first question–what is a proper brief? Some designers see briefs as problems waiting to be solved; others see them as a springboard to produce a highly individualistic response. But I've always found it helpful to regard a brief as a *question in need of an answer*. I like this approach because if we are going to come up with an answer, we have to understand the question. I mean really *understand* it.

For graphic designers, the need to interrogate every brief we are given is paramount. If we don't query everything that is put in front of us, we run the risk of being compliant and submissive, and these are two qualities that are not conducive to creativity; they are the qualities of mediocrity. And yet by urging the adoption of a questioning attitude, I'm not advocating a carping or complaining approach. Rather, I'm saying that we should be sceptical (but not accusatory) about what we are told by clients; we should be wary of conventional wisdom, but not dismissive of common sense. Genuinely creative people do this anyway. They don't mind appearing oppositional and argumentative, and perhaps it's this contrarian instinct that makes people suspicious–frightened, even–of creative people.

Here's another thing about briefs–there is nearly always something missing from them, and that *missing something* is usually the key to unlocking the brief. This is just as well, because if design briefs held all the answers there would be no need for creative thought: clients would tell designers what to do and pay them to deliver pre-packed solutions.

Here's an example of what I mean. I was once part of a team invited to bid for the redesign of a property magazine. It was a journal for the professional sector of the UK real-estate market, and it was read by developers, investors, architects, and property conglomerates. The magazine had previously received a full-scale graphic makeover by a leading international design company, but was now showing its age. An exhaustive and detailed brief was supplied. My colleagues and I sifted through the well-written document and discussed it in detail. We analyzed it. We tried to condense it. We looked for the missing element.

The brief stated that a redesign was necessary because the existing design was dated. It pointed out that various navigational improvements were required to reflect the magazine's changing editorial makeup. And it listed some requirements concerning the accommodation of new features and advertising. The brief went into copious and helpful detail about its readership and its competitors on the newsstands.

But we sensed that there was something missing from the brief.

It was only by relentlessly interrogating the magazine's art director and editor that the missing part was identified. The property market, it was explained to us, had changed dramatically in recent years. It used to be a business for rich men with cigars, pinstripe suits, and Rolls-Royces. Today, it has become a much less formal business, populated by younger people of both sexes, many of whom wear informal clothes to work, and who value design (interior design, product design, and architecture) as an essential part of the property-development process. We'd noticed that printed literature and billboards put up by property companies and developers had become "stylish." The property world, we noted, had woken up to good design.

Here was the missing component that gave us our winning formula. We based our response on the idea that the magazine's new design had to combine informality with high contemporary style, while continuing to function as a digest of news and comment, with its attendant production and editorial demands. In our presentation, we convinced the publisher, the editor, the advertising manager, and the art director that this was the right answer to the question posed in the brief. But that insight wasn't in the brief—like a lost contact lens in the long grass, *we had to go looking for it.*

## The bad brief

To be asked to do a design job without a proper brief is a bad thing, and yet even when we get a brief, our problems are not necessarily over. Design briefs are often shoddy, half-baked, and unpromising.[2] But this only means that we have to fight to make them into "good briefs." Sometimes we will push too hard and come into conflict with our client and end up getting the sack. On other occasions, we will succeed, and turn a base-metal brief into a block of shining gold.

2   It was common when showing Intro work at design events and art colleges to be asked how we managed to get so many "good briefs." This made me splutter. We didn't get "good briefs," we got the same shoddy briefs everyone else gets; we just made them good by questioning them, challenging them, and sometimes disobeying them.

**How to be a graphic designer, without losing your soul**

The first thing to do is start with the premise that even a bad brief is really a good brief. I'd go so far as to say that assuming a sound moral and ethical base (we are not, for example, being asked to design a web site for a company with a history of dumping toxic waste), there is no such thing as a bad brief, only a bad response. But let's assume that our client has given us a comprehensive, well-thought-out document stating all the requirements of the job, and that we have agreed the schedule and budget. What happens next? Well, written briefs do not preclude us from having further discussions with our client about the project. This will throw up interesting information and reveal nuances perhaps not covered in the document. It will also allow us to test our preliminary thinking on our client.

Naturally, we must fully absorb the written brief, and we must avoid concentrating on the bits we like the look of or those bits that give us the chance to do what we do best. Instead, we must look for problem areas and confront those parts of the brief that force us to ask questions such as—do we need external help with this project? Is it beyond our capabilities? Also, if we are working with a team, we need to go through it with group members and make sure we all see it in the same way (this is often difficult to achieve since others can get snared and snagged on different aspects of the project).

But there's worse—sometimes briefs are simply wrong, and it is occasionally necessary to disobey them. "Wrong" briefs make false assumptions and outline premises that are incorrect, feeble, or short-sighted. When we spot this, we have a choice. We can walk away, or we can do what is asked of us. But there's another option, and that is to disobey the brief and do what we think is right. With this approach we risk everything: we risk incurring the client's displeasure, and we risk being sacked from a project. Yet if we are confident that we are right, and can live with the consequences, it's often worth a bit of old-fashioned disobedience.

There is a great example of disobeying a "wrong" brief in the work of Bruno Monguzzi, the great Swiss designer. He was called in by the Musée d'Orsay in Paris, after a design competition had failed to produce a winning poster with which to launch the newly opened museum. Monguzzi was instructed to design a poster avoiding pictorial imagery and using only two elements: the museum logo (which Monguzzi had designed) and the date. Monguzzi describes his response:

"So here I was at home with a new brief and began to endlessly play around with the date and the logo, the logo and the date, getting nowhere. Nothing was happening, nothing was opening, nothing was beginning. I walked over to my books, picked up a [Henri] Lartigue album, and slowly began to go through the pages. When I came to the image of his brother taking off with a glider that their uncle had constructed at Château de Rouzat, I knew I had the answer. The fly had broken the web.

"And here I was, back in Paris again, with Jean Jenger [the director] and Leone Nora [public relations], knowing I had disobeyed. I was using a photograph, and no image was to be used. Jenger got very upset. He said that we had all agreed that no work of art should appear on the poster. And that anyway it was not 'le musée de l'aviation.'

"I said that it was a metaphor and that the people that knew the logo knew what the museum was all about. I nevertheless added that the poster had to be their poster. That it should belong to them. But Jenger had stopped listening and began to talk to himself pacing nervously up and down the room. I tried to interrupt him, asserting that he did not have to convince me. He said he was thinking. My eyes met the eyes of Madame Nora, which were a bit perplexed, but very beautiful, and we sat down.

"Jenger would sometimes stop, look at the poster, and then start his gymnastics all over again. I think he was trying to imagine the possible reactions of all the people he really or virtually knew. A kind of French human comedy with an unexpected end. 'Monguzzi', he said, 'I am so convinced that the poster is right, that I will bring it myself to Rigaud' [the president of the museum]. The following day a worried Madame Nora was on the phone. The Lartigue Foundation does not allow the cropping of Lartigue's photographs. Not knowing which way to turn I asked her to try showing the project to the Foundation anyway. Not only were we allowed to use the photograph as planned, but a vintage print of that shot was given to the museum. It was the fourth Lartigue to enter the collection."[3]

There are two important lessons to be gleaned from this extract. The first is that it is sometimes necessary to disobey a brief when we know it to be wrong. It was clear that the museum director was wrong—or at best short-sighted—to prohibit the use of pictorial imagery and impose restrictions on the designer. (It almost certainly explains why the competition entries were all regarded as worthless—they'd followed the brief and were consequently bloodless and ineffectual.) By disregarding the brief, Monguzzi produced an enduring piece of work that would have had much less impact if he'd followed his client's instructions.

The second lesson is less obvious. In this account of his experience of designing a poster, Monguzzi illustrates the need to give new work time to become assimilated by the client. As I pointed out in Chapter 7, designers often expect instant responses to their work when clients really need time to absorb and reflect upon it. The client brings his or her own expectations to any work they are seeing for the first time. These expectations have to be sifted through before an objective and considered response can be formulated. The museum director went from disapproval to enthusiastic acceptance, but he didn't do it instantly. Monguzzi knew to give him time.

3   Taken from *Bruno Monguzzi, A Designer's Perspective*, Baltimore: The Fine Arts Gallery, 1998.

### Self-initiated briefs

The notion of self-initiated briefs—personal work or graphic authorship, as it is sometimes called —currently occupies a prominent position in design discourse. Yet, in my experience, some of the poorest work produced by graphic designers is undertaken under the banner of self-initiated briefs. This is not to say that I don't believe that there is a role for graphic authorship, or that there are benefits to be derived from self-initiated briefs. It is rather that only a few graphic designers have a genuine aptitude for self-initiated work; due to education, temperament, and tradition, the designer's mentality is usually better suited to *responding* to an external brief, not *initiating* it.

**How to be a graphic designer, without losing your soul**

Yet I would never try to dissuade anyone from writing their own brief, doing their own personal work, or attempting graphic authorship. If graphic design is to become a more valued profession, it needs designers who can think and write, and generate their own ideas. The modern designer has a skill set—especially in the area of digital capabilities—that makes it possible to challenge the old notion of the designer as passive hired help waiting by the phone for the next job to turn up.

With the recognition of "design thinking" as a new, valuable, and potent tool, designers are starting to move up the food chain in the eyes of many policy-makers. Today, the modern designer can be anything he or she wants: entrepreneurs (especially in the digital realm), publishers, moviemakers, vendors of designer artifacts, typefaces, and apps. In reality, designers are so crucial to the success of most commercial activities, it is a wonder that more designers haven't realized their importance: imagine Apple without Jonathan Ive.

But I come back to my belief that most designers are not at their best when responding to a self-written brief. Designers need constraints; they may moan about restrictions, and yearn to work unmolested by client interference—but like a prisoner released from jail after decades inside, they rarely know what to do when confronted with freedom.

Designers with an itch to experiment, and designers who burn to do the sort of work they are prevented from doing in their daily lives, often imagine that a self-initiated brief is the answer to their need. It might be. Writing, editing, and designing a book on a favorite subject, or starting a web site with personal content, might be an excellent idea—or it might be an orgy of self-indulgence and self-absorption. A much niftier idea might be to scout around for a real live brief: perhaps a charity or a good cause, something that enables us to show moral as well as creative support. A real live brief effectively executed will carry more value than a self-initiated one, and will have the added bonus of giving the designer an aid to find a better job, or to attract better clients. Self-initiated briefs may be good for the soul, and they may have a benefit as a sort of creative gym, but they are rarely taken seriously by employers or potential clients.

### The myth of originality

We can't look at creativity without mentioning a fixation that has a great influence on the way designers function in the post-modern world where everything, seemingly, has already been done. I'm talking about the concept of originality. Most designers are untroubled by the notion of originality, but others are obsessed with it, and many problems are caused by the quest for originality. In my view, originality is a misunderstood quality in contemporary graphic design. Copying is bad, no question. Infringing someone's copyright (stealing their work or their ideas) for personal gain is immoral, not to mention illegal in most countries. But the only people who copy are the terminally second-rate and the downright dishonest—and they always get found out.

Too often, an obsession with originality leads to a sort of creative timidity. The bold designer, on the other hand, borrows freely and adapts from sources in precisely the way artists have done for centuries. Furthermore, good designers readily admit to this "appropriation." It is a quality of many top designers that their influences and sources are clearly visible and readily acknowledged. Copyists never own up—either to themselves or to others (and especially not to the people they are aping)—and that's a big point of difference between the talented designer and the third-rater.

But let's not kid ourselves that day-of-creation originality is possible in graphic design. Designers are locked into an interconnecting matrix of tradition and shared sensibility. Design mostly deals with an accepted code of images, signs, and symbols, which we are required to use as part of the tools of our daily life. After all, an arrow is an arrow, and if we deviate too far from its graphic purity we may end up sending someone in the wrong direction. Or worse.

All designers can hope to do is acquire a voice that they can call their own. But a voice, paradoxically, is most readily acquired by opening ourselves up to the influence of other schools of design and visual art. My personal philosophy is that it is right to borrow and to be influenced by visual material as long as we are not slavishly copying it, and as long as we use our sources to make something demonstrably new.

The British designer Julian House, who I worked with closely for a number of years, has clear views on this question. In a conversation I had with him he said "I don't believe in originality as an absolute." "I think it's more to do with interesting twists on existing forms. Borrowing from the Modernist designers of the recent past, for instance, is not plagiarism; it's more a continuation of the processes and ideas that they set in motion. I'm influenced by Polish poster art of the 1960s, which was influenced by Pop Art and Surrealism, and which in turn freely appropriated commercial art, comic book art, cinema, and Victorian engravings. I think the key to whether it's good or not lies in the viewer's response to a piece of design. Do they say 'I've seen it before' or, 'I've seen it before but not in that way.'"

In other words, it is acceptable to borrow from, for example, the Victorian illustrator Aubrey Beardsley, as the English psychedelic poster artists did in the late 1960s, just so long as something new emerges from it. Picasso did it with African masks; in his use of these beautiful images he performed an act of transformation that allowed us to see something new.

Welcoming influences into our work is one of the ways in which we expand our creative range. Designers enrich their work—not diminish it—by looking for ways to "incorporate" new and radical modes of expression into their work, especially from places outside contemporary design. Shutting out influences because of an obsession with "originality" is a trap.

## The creative process

I always begin any creative task by searching for a mood or atmosphere. Every situation has its own "atmosphere": it might be serious, playful, nostalgic, or utterly pragmatic, and once I've found it I start to inhabit that emotional or aesthetic location. I have to "feel" the project in the way a visitor might "feel" a new country. To understand a new place we have to absorb it, breathe it in—we must inhale.

**How to be a graphic designer, without losing your soul**

This works for me, but creative people function in different ways: some begin a new project by tidying their desks; others work in ever-increasing chaos; some plunge in— sketching, scanning, grabbing, downloading; others go off for a period of reflection, reading, and careful analysis. There is no correct way to start a creative journey. Each of us must find a way that suits us. But in the age of the deadline, when every project, big or small, is marked *urgent*, how do we find a way of approaching our creative work that ensures a successful outcome?

Graphic design is now almost entirely a digital activity: as designers, we need never again hold a pencil or develop a photographic print from a negative, or create a font by hand. It can all be done with a computer. The computer has revolutionized the design process. It has made the act of designing easier, and in many ways it has improved the way we design things. Yet in other respects it has made design more formulaic; it has standardized the act of designing and it has standardized the output of designers.

Today, thanks to speed-of-light microprocessors and do-everything software, we all design in the same way: we sit, nearly motionless, only our wrists moving as we stare at our screens. Our focus has narrowed. We rarely look at our work from a distance. We rarely look at it from different angles. We often work in miniature. We avoid anything that can't be done "on" the computer. The screen dictates our relationship to our work; it dictates how our work looks. It's why all the good studios I know pin stuff up on a wall and look at it from varying distances and varying angles. This is vital if we are doing a poster, signage, or anything that is seen at a distance greater than arm's length—but it applies to most forms of graphic output, too.

I'm not anti-computer. Far from it. The computer enables us to do more work, and it enables us to operate with greater technical proficiency. It has freed the designer from drudgery. It has brought modes of graphic expression that were once nearly impossible to achieve because of cost or technical complexity within the grasp of any designer who can afford a computer. The computer is a good thing. No question about it. But with the computer has come a set of problems that, virus-like, infect the actual process of design. What used to be slow and methodical is now fast and often slipshod: ask a designer to produce logo ideas and you'll get dozens of versions in roughly the time it takes to think them into existence.

The computer allows the designer to explore countless options. Before computers, designers had to trace off letterforms, or hand-render text, or represent pictures with Magic Marker sketches; it might have taken an entire morning to render a headline, or days to prepare a mock-up of a typographic layout, or months to create a typeface. Neville Brody tells the story of the epiphany-like moment when he saw, for the first time, Fontographer being used to create a font. Up until this point, Brody had been laboriously drawing alphabets by hand (as had been the case for centuries), but now here was a way that meant it could be done in a fraction of the time. Brody became a digital convert. He was among the first high-profile converts to the computer in design.

But with speed of execution comes another problem—a very digital problem. With the ability to produce so much work, it's harder to know whether what we are doing is any good. Ian Anderson, the self-taught graphic designer and founder of The Designers Republic, was asked if he ever suffered from designer's block: "My problem in that area," he noted, "and it sounds an arrogant thing to say, is there are too many ideas, and information overload. Then it's how do I get everything I want to say into this thing. I can't remember a time when I didn't know what to do or didn't know how to do it. It's much more about which route to take. If you have a block you should just walk around it or start your own journey from a different place. Looking at something in a different way requires the discipline of giving up what you already have. Sometimes the only way to move forward is to dump everything and start again. Then you will find the work you have already completed helps inform your new direction." [4]

Nick Long (ed.), S-Book 2, Art Books International, 2004. [4]

Anderson has touched on a uniquely digital problem facing the contemporary designer. He is talking about the importance of the designer's role as "editor." Editing is the great skill of the digital era. Now that we can produce a surfeit of everything, the ability to know what to retain and what to discard is essential. In the digital domain we can have everything we want. With digital cameras we can incorporate images within seconds. With scanners we can scan anything that can be fitted onto a scanner bed. We can have any typeface. Any effect. And we can have it now. So when Anderson talks about taking alternative "routes," starting journeys from a "different place," dumping everything, and starting again, he is really talking about editing.

How do you edit? To be a good editor, you need time, detachment, and judgement. By all means create thirty logos before lunchtime, but never show thirty logos to a client; show only three, or at most four versions. Showing more reveals us to be indecisive (no editing skills) and creates a picture of graphic design as a scattergun process. And here's another thing—don't send them until the following day. Print them out, pin them on the wall, and go home. Come back the next day, and we will see things that we didn't see yesterday. Ask friends and other designers what they think.

Ian Anderson also alludes to another process that is a direct by-product of the digital way of working: iteration. Digital tools allow the designer to "iterate" on a grand scale. "Thirty logos by end of the day? No problem. Color and mono versions in varying sizes? No problem. They'll be loaded onto an FTP site by 5.00pm. Call me when you've seen them." This is business in real time. It's what the modern world is about. If we can't do thirty logos by 5.00pm for our client in Singapore, someone else will. But hang on, what about quality?

Many designers use iteration as a sort of mechanism to avoid failure. If I produce thirty logos—300 even  then my client is bound to like one of them. Surely? Not necessarily. Unless we apply careful editing as we go, we will end up with a soup of indifferent ideas, remarkable only for their plentifulness. And we are also sending a bad signal to our clients: we are saying we don't really know what we are doing. Instead, we must use iteration to work toward a conclusion rather than as an opportunity to explore every known avenue. In the pre-digital era, the designer had to think harder about the final destination, because iteration wasn't possible on any scale. Few of us would go back to that way of working, but we must learn to structure our work so that we progress in a straight line rather than a serpentine loop that never arrives anywhere.

**How to be a graphic designer, without losing your soul**

Criteria for good work

What constitutes good work? For one designer, a handpainted sign on a fruit stall in Mumbai is the pinnacle of graphic excellence. For another, it is the modular typography of Wim Crouwel. For others it is design that delivers a successful message, and for some it is design that has aesthetic or ethical integrity. So what is the correct answer? In the original version of this book, I thought that the answer to this question was as follows: there are three questions to ask ourselves at the end of every job. Is the client happy? Is the job profitable? Is the project newsworthy? If we can answer yes to all three questions, the result will be "good work."

I wrote the above words at a time shortly after I was released from the daily task of running a design studio. In my head, I was still fretting over the need to do interesting work but also hit our monthly sales targets (a pretty scary figure when you are twenty-five-strong that even now, six years later, makes me shudder). But now that I no longer run a studio, these criteria seem selfish and narrow. What about the end user? I can't believe I didn't mention the end user. And what about the ethical position?

Well, let's look again at my original three criteria (they still stand), but this time let's add the poor end user and the ethical position.

Is the client happy? This is pretty crucial when we think about it. If the client is unhappy, we've got a problem. It might simply mean that we don't get any more work from that client, and it will almost certainly mean that we won't get any recommendations or referrals from them either. At worst, it might mean that we don't get paid: if it's a big job, with a large fee involved and substantial outside costs, this might be catastrophic. And perhaps most painful of all, we will know that we have failed professionally. The professional nature of design means that we are obliged to make our clients happy, and to fail to do this is to fail professionally. Just think of all those letters to newspapers complaining about malpractice in financial institutions: if we screw up professionally, we are no better than the insurance conglomerate that fails to pay out a policy on a technicality or due to incompetence.

Is the job profitable? Profitability can be measured in many ways—we may lose money on a job, for example, but it may open a door for us that leads to new opportunities. Yet in the term's strictly financial sense, it means not losing money on a job and showing a cash profit. If we want to survive in the design business and be able to pay our taxes, our staff, and ourselves, we are going to have to show a profit on most of our jobs, although not necessarily on every job. But we are going to have to make more money than we spend. Capitalism may be far from perfect, but it has a simplicity that is easily grasped.

Is the project newsworthy? What I'm talking about here is our work's ability to attract attention and, as a consequence, attract other work. In the current design scene nothing succeeds like success. It gets people talking (word of mouth), it excites journalists and commentators (exposure), and it wins awards and gets published in books and exhibitions (recognition).

Okay, so what about the "end user"? What about our "target audience"? Surely they are of supreme importance in establishing the criteria for success. Well, yes and no. I realize now that I neglected to mention the end user first time round for two reasons. The first is that consideration for the end user is so ingrained in the designer's psychology that, like breathing, we hardly think it is worth mentioning. To be a good designer we have to put ourselves into the heads of our target audience. When we do this, we become the end user. The second reason is more problematical. Designers often end up seeing their clients as the target audience. In truth, we rarely get to meet the people who are the recipients of our work. Instead, since our clients are the gatekeepers between us and them, they often become proxy end users and we end up confusing them with the actual end user. But they are not: the end user is the end user.

The final criterion is the ethical dimension. It is no longer enough to say that we have done a good job, made some money, and got a write-up on a few hot design blogs. Today, our work has to be based on the principles of sustainability and ethical foundations. I say *has* to, and of course we are free to not bother about either sustainability or ethics. But we ignore these issues at our peril. A new generation of clients—and designers—is emerging who demand that we take heed of these factors. Public tenders—a growing source of work for designers all over the world—now routinely insist on adherence to ethical and environmental practices. 5

Of course, there will always be work for uncaring designers and studios that don't give a hoot about ethical concerns. But as more and more clients—in both public and private sectors—build environmental and ethical conditions into their terms and conditions, it will become less and less easy to avoid our responsibilities in this area. I have said more about this in Chapter 8, where I look at the question of ethics and sustainability in graphic design.

5 I recently took part in a major, and much publicized, bid for a public works design project. The forms that entrants were required to complete contained questions relating to applicants' employment policies on race, gender, and disability. All forms were scored on the responses to these and other questions. A poor score would result in dismissal, regardless of creative submissions.

## Conclusion

Having finished reading this book, it is my arrogant hope that readers feel better equipped to deal with life as a graphic designer. The subject is vast, and I can only aspire to dealing with one tiny sliver of the cake. I haven't talked about design theory or the minutiae of practice life (job numbers, project management, or tax planning). There are better people than me to write about these subjects, and I've provided a bibliography with recommendations for further reading. But just as research and inquisitiveness should be a big part of our life as a designer, so should a willingness to learn.

**How to be a graphic designer, without losing your soul**

When I started life as a designer it seemed to me to be the most exciting job in the world. I still feel that. There's something uniquely privileged and stimulating about having a job where we know we will have an effect (however slight) on the lives of others; there's something magical about doing something that might be seen by millions; and there's something exhilarating about having a job where we have the potential to make the world a better place—if only slightly.

The biggest problem designers face is fear: fear of clients, fear of failure, fear of ideas. Our ability to overcome fear is perhaps the greatest skill we can acquire. Most bad design, most mediocre design, is a consequence of fear. Clients are frightened; designers are frightened; audiences are frightened. The modern world of commerce runs on fear: a marketplace terror that makes us timid and risk-averse. Most of us deal with fear by falling back on the familiar and the safe. But if we do this, we are not allowed to turn round and say our lives are dull. If we are going to avoid losing our souls, we have to overcome the fear.

**How to be a graphic designer, without losing your soul**

Jonathan Barnbrook on graphic design and ethics

Jonathan Barnbrook is a British graphic designer and typeface designer widely known for his commitment to political and ethical thinking in design. In the past, oppositional movements shunned formal graphic design and turned instead to more anarchic modes of expression. But Barnbrook brings the refinement and elegance of classical graphic design to the task of exposing such topics as US bombing statistics and corporate malfeasance. He does this by creating his own hybrid style of neo-classicism mixed with digital avant-gardism, and by "fighting advertising or political messages from politicians with their own tools." His is one of the most singular and recognizable voices in modern graphic design.

barnbrook.net

Project
Exocet font
Client
Emigre
Designer
Jonathan Barnbrook
Date
1991

AS:    Can you begin by describing what sort of graphic designer you are?

JB:    Hmmm.... There are several strands to my work. First, I try to be a problem-solver, to communicate clearly. I get very excited by trying to take a complex idea and expressing it simply. This I think is the traditional way designers are seen.

Second, I try to be a problem-revealer to use design to highlight and explain problems that we face as a society and hopefully to engage people in doing something about it. This is the reason I do political work. I collaborate with charities and people like Adbusters. The reason I choose "graphic design" to do this is because it doesn't have the pretence of many other visual professions; it's essentially valueless and is made for mass production. In this desire to be a *problem-revealer* I also want to be positive, not just complain—either to make people see there are pathways out of a situation or that we can look at things in a different way from the traditional one.

Finally, I realized that my major interest in design comes from the influence of psycho-geography—the effect on the emotions and states of mind of your geographical environment. Graphic design is one of the major ways this is transmitted to me. It can be an old sign somewhere or the small details you see when you go to a new city; we all react emotionally to these things, in a way often quite unintended by the designer. I try to put these feelings in particular into my typefaces. It's quite hard to explain—feelings of nostalgia, ennui, some quite painful, some to do with a beauty that has been lost, but they are all because of the ephemeral and prominent nature of design. There is an attempt in my work to express it to other people. This is the one where I hope to connect in a different, less quantifiable, logical way.

You're well known as a designer of typefaces. Some of your fonts have become pop culture classics and turn up in the oddest places.[1] Is there a difference between the sensibility required to be a typeface designer—and in your case, vendor too—and the sensibility required to be a graphic designer for hire? I think for me it was one of intensity, of what you are prepared to put into the work. I became a type designer because as a graphic designer I wanted to go deeper into the subject. I could take the photos, design the page, and write the text. But drawing the font as well gave me more control. It meant you could affect the voice of the text absolutely and create a universe that was unique in the work.

[1]    The Barnbrook-designed typeface Priori Serif is used in the title sequence for *University Challenge*, the long-running and popular BBC TV quiz show.

I think, though, that being a type designer means you have to learn your craft a bit more deeply, and you definitely have to know the history. I think it's fairly easy to do average graphic design with not much skill involved. But it really shows when you are a type designer. There are so many aspects to consider—comparisons of weight, spacing, elegance. I'm not saying it's easier, just that it can be easier to get away with design without so much knowledge.

The attraction to typography is that you can be subversive by minimal means. It's fascinating playing with the model that people have in their heads of a letterform, and it has a very interesting creative history, which people get annoyed about if you muck about with—which is, of course, the best reason to do it. Also there is always the thrill of being able to type anything that a human being has written in your own typeface. It's a wonderful thing.

**How to be a graphic designer, without losing your soul**

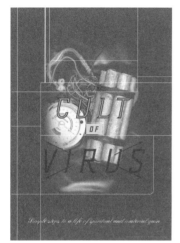

Project
Virusfonts Catalogue
Designer
Jonathan Barnbrook
Date
1997

There's always been a political dimension to your work. Where does your interest in political campaigning come from? It comes from my working-class background. Both my parents worked in car factories, and in that situation you need to pressurize the employers, whoever they are, to give you better rights because nobody is going to give you anything. It made me realize that that kind of pressure does have an effect. It might be a small one, but if there are enough people involved then change does happen.

Also, we have this incredibly powerful tool in our hands, but most people choose to ignore the power it has to change society and affect opinions. If this is not the case, why are we surrounded by advertising hoardings, bombarded with TV commercials, and given leaflets to sell us stuff? It is exactly the same media that is used to facilitate change in protest and political movements. So I am confident that design has that power. It's just that we are distracted so much by well-paying "glam" jobs that people think it's not realistic to use it in this way. It's only designers who get hung up about whether a poster can change things or not. The non-designers are out there using it already as one of many things in their arsenal to put over their messages.

One or two commentators have described you as angry. Until I met you, I had the same feeling. But in person you give the impression of being good-natured and well-balanced. Are you an angry person? Well, I think it's more a case that most people are too scared or apathetic to say anything, so anybody who makes the effort and says something "real" is seen as standing out.

I can understand why I am seen as "angry," because of the direct nature of the statements in the work, but they need to be direct for people to get the message. Design and language are the weapons I use, but that is not the only aspect of what I do.

I don't act "angry," but I am not so happy with the world I live in. I want it to be better, and there is a good way to go about it and a bad way. I think to be a good designer you *must* be able to get on with people and discuss things in a civil way; you must love other human beings, which I do. There is no point in saying something worthwhile in your work if you act like a jerk when you talk to people about it. And there is no point in talking about issues that affect us all if you don't respect the people you are talking to.

Your political work has helped you become extremely well-known within design, but has it hindered you professionally in any way? Some people have seen it as a move to get publicity to be successful. I would not be this calculating—it would be completely disingenuous. Cynicism is one of the worst blights in graphic design, and it seems to mean that most people sit on their arses and criticize without making an effort or realizing that they can change things. I do it because I don't think it's acceptable to work for things you don't believe in.

So yes, it has hindered us a great deal. I am sure I could be a rich person if I didn't do socially engaged projects, but if I have enough to survive on then I would rather be doing the work that I care about than having a comfortable life saying absolutely zero, and it is central to the idea of your "soul" as a designer. There is a bit of me that would die if I were coerced to tell lies. There is room for everybody to say and design what they want to, but the first thing is to realize the possibilities and not self-censor.

Project
**Adbusters Billboard**
Client
**Adbusters**
Designer
**Jonathan Barnbrook**
Date
**2001**

Project
**David Bowie,**
**Heathen album cover**
Client
**ISO/Columbia**
Designer
**Jonathan Barnbrook**
Photographer
**Marcus Klinko**
Date
**2001**

**How to be a graphic designer, without losing your soul**

I think most companies are scared to work with us because of the political work. I can understand why, because most of them don't actually like designers with a strong opinion. When anything "subversive" is used by a company it immediately has any contentious content removed. They want to be sure that designers are kept as part of a service industry. That is why it is so difficult to move the design profession forward; we are all too scared and too conditioned not to make waves.

I do wish that I were given bigger projects to work on. This is a problem of perception, too. Often the huge projects go to the big boring design companies because they are perceived as being "able to handle it," but actually some of the best work in design has been done by individuals overseeing a small group of people who have been the overseers of a project.

Unlike a great many politically motivated designers, your work has an unmistakable polish and finesse—you don't chuck your work together randomly. Is there a sense in which you are bringing the polish and finesse of modern visual communication—branding and commercial messages, for example—to your political work? I think it would be dishonest to do something that looks homemade or kind of DIY graphics because, although that is what is often associated with activism, it is not my background. If I have a skill I would like to use it to be as effective as possible. I understand the process of a good copy line in advertising, of an arresting visual, and especially a simple idea to grab people's attention, so it's very much fighting advertising or messages from politicians with their own tools. It's a much better way to work.

For some reason I am often called a "style merchant." I have never understood this, because yes, I like the work to look right, but there would be no work if I weren't trying to say something with it. It's the form follows function idea, which actually has nothing to do with function and more to do with taste.

What can a graphic designer hope to achieve by dedicating themselves to a course of political action? Or to put it another way, what is the role of graphic design in political action?

Well, I think they should not see themselves as a graphic designer being political but as a citizen of society putting their talent to good use. So I don't think it's a question of deciding to be engaged or not.

Anyway, to get back to the question, graphic design is one of the methods used to convey the message and inform people of what you are trying to say. It is hugely important. We should not forget that graphic design started when people scribbled on a wall something that they wanted other people to know about (and the reason why we will go out and flypost [wheatpasting] when we feel strongly about something). It has a very basic function to inform in the simplest way possible, and as such is used as a major way of "getting the message out." It seems that this acknowledgment of power other than in commercial terms has the weight of design education and designers' egos against it. The short-termism and narrow-mindedness in design education is a real problem, from both colleges and students; there is too much emphasis on getting a commercial job when there are so many different paths a student can follow. Also, there is real opposition in the design industry to the idea that graphic design has a role to play in change. It's astounding when all people have to do is to take a wider view of design history to see this is the case. I suspect it's a combination of laziness and lack of accountability.

You are a strong-minded designer with talent and a powerful vision of how you want to live and work. But what would you say to someone starting out who perhaps didn't have your talent or singular vision, yet wanted to live and work ethically and have a political voice? Well, it is never simple and I still don't approach a piece of work and think that I can solve it easily. I think it's not good to think you are "talented" or anything special at all really. First, I would say that one of the biggest problems people seem to have is feeling strongly about something. There is too much onus on passivity, to expect things to happen to us rather than be active. If you don't have a clue what you want to do, just *start somewhere*—it will reveal itself sooner or later.

Second, try not to be distracted—life has a way of intervening in your plans, and I see so many students getting distracted.

The third thing is to work properly and seriously and to take an obsessive interest in every aspect of your profession.

Fourth, if you are doing political work, fact-check, fact-check, fact-check—don't trust the Internet.

Fifth, there is no point in doing something about the environment or politics if it just stays in your portfolio; that has no impact and is inauthentic. You have to go out and engage with people who are politically active. You will find it rewarding and they will value your input into the process.

Sixth, the local school could need your design help, which is as important as your big message about how to save humanity, so think practically if you want to do work that has an effect on people.

Seventh, have a sense of humor about yourself in any situation. It will help in many different ways.

Finally, most things are quite simple, although people would tell you many reasons why they are not.

In 2007 you published the book *Barnbrook Bible*, a 330-page monograph and a majorly ambitious project. Many designers would give a few gallons of blood to have this opportunity. Can you say what it means to you professionally and personally? I didn't really think about it being something that other designers would like to do, or to get some kind of ego boost. It was first and foremost to explain the work and to motivate other designers, especially students. I wanted to let them know that there should be reasons for designing your work a certain way and it's important to be able to articulate them. Also that you could survive being politically or socially engaged.

There was also a desire for people outside design to be able to see that there were people working in our profession who had something to say—that design should be treated as a serious subject. I never had an idea to have a career in design or to be "famous"; both seem a little bit contrived. All I have tried to do is be honest in my work. Everything else has been a consequence. So I hope the book most of all shows that if you are honest you can find space to do the work you want to do.

**How to be a graphic designer, without losing your soul**

Ben Drury on graphic design and design for music

Ben Drury made his reputation and acquired his cult following as art director of the record label Mo' Wax. Working with label founder and DJ James Lavelle, Drury created a lasting body of work that caught the freewheeling spirit of both the music and the era. He worked closely with legendary artist Futura 2000 to produce the book *Futura*, which was published in 2000. He has collaborated with Nike on numerous signature products, and today he works with leading UK musicians such as Dizzee Rascal and UNKLE. In 2008 he left London to live in the English countryside with his wife and young family.

thesilentlistener.com

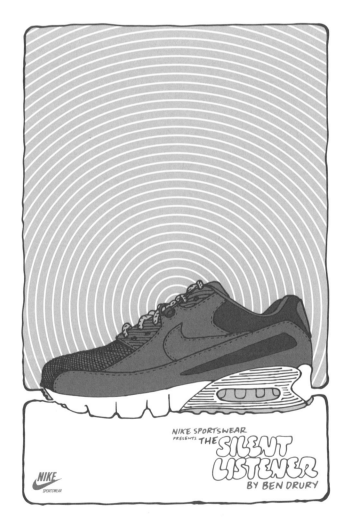

Project
Nike promotional
poster for
Drury Airmax
Client
Nike
Designer
Ben Drury
Illustrator
Ben Drury
Date
2009

AS:    What attracted you to graphic design in the first place?

BD:    I had a natural aptitude for art, which I think really helps. As a child I was very aware of being part of a designed world, fascinated by why some things looked better than others. I would always get better marks when there was an element of design involved—maps, graphs, lettering, etc.

Were there things you were taught at design school that you didn't see the benefit of until later? Only that if I had wanted to go to the RCA to do an M.A., I probably should have worked harder. I was too busy on other things, including doing *real* jobs for *real* clients.

Would you recommend working on live commercial projects to today's students? And what do you think you got out of it? Of course. You can only learn so much from virtual problem-solving in the classroom, so the sooner you engage with the world the better.

Tell me about how you got into music design. Through a love of music, which informed my love of hanging about in record shops. It was never my intention to become a designer who exclusively works in the music industry, though.

Besides the freedom and the once-in-a-lifetime projects that you worked on at Mo' Wax, what else did you learn from this experience? Nothing ever lasts forever.

Were there any downsides? For example, do you think you missed something by not working for one of the big design companies or would that have stifled you? I'm not sure what you mean by "big design companies." I certainly wasn't out for fame and glory. I just followed my instincts, which were always to keep it small. The designers I was inspired by all had names, they weren't companies, although if I had done a bit more reading and stopped looking at the pictures I would have realized that all of them had teams of people supporting them and enabling them to work on much larger projects for much bigger clients.

The idea of working as a small cog within a large machine never really appealed to me, although I think I would have liked more structure and guidance at certain points. I always wanted a manager. I approached my practice as a solo musician would. When I started out, I was part of a duo (with Will Bankhead), but then we went our own separate ways... we still collaborate occasionally.

Why do you think album covers and music-related design has such an enduring appeal for designers? Free gigs? Free records? I don't really know. It's exciting I suppose; there are fewer conventions to adhere to, a more open-minded audience, and working with interesting like-minded creative people. Any of these reasons apply, but in my experience all of them could also be proved to be fantasy. At its best, when it all comes together as it should, there's a beautiful synergy between the art and the music that makes it a very satisfying experience.

What do you say to designers who want to do music design in light of what is happening to music packaging in the download era? We've talked about this in the past and I've had a very negative outlook, but in light of some recent experiences my viewpoint has shifted. Recorded music will always be accompanied by some sort of graphic; it's only the method of delivery that is changing.

You have become known as one of the leading music industry designers. Has this been a hindrance in any way? Has it stopped you being asked to design other sorts of work, for example? The borders of music design have been very clearly defined and I do think it's difficult for potential clients (unless they too are in the music industry) to make that leap of faith between the perceived frivolity of graphics for music and, for example, the graphics for a new car launch. I take what I do seriously and the skills I have are totally transferable to any other area that requires art direction or design.

## How to be a graphic designer, without losing your soul

You are involved in designing trainers for Nike. How does this work come to you —was it an extension of your music work? Nike approached me a few years ago to be part of a project they were working on, celebrating ten years of their Airmax range. It was to design a pair of trainers, jacket, tee, etc. It went down really well and they've been coming back ever since. I've just completed a three-way collaboration between myself, Nike, and Dizzee Rascal, which has been great fun. It all happened alongside the release of his latest album, so I treated the trainer and its promotional video as integrated elements of the same campaign. It's a similar approach to how we did things at Mo' Wax. When it works, it's great.

You talked about your skills being "transferable," but you always give the impression of being more like an artist than a jobbing graphic designer. Is this accurate? I'm not sure what impression I give. The art vs. commerce debate is difficult for me. Obviously I have transferable skills because I've learnt a lot over the years, and I'll apply whichever of those skills a specific job requires. The fact that I get paid for (most of) my work and that it's for a client defines me as a commercial artist. I definitely lean towards an old-school design approach—more in the tradition of artist/designer/craftsmen like Saul Bass, Abram Games, Milton Glaser, or Bruno Munari, who seemed to glide effortlessly between disciplines—than rigidly adhering to systems and grids. I'm happy to be called a "designer."

Can you talk about your website—www.thesilentlistener.com? I've been neglecting it recently, so I feel guilty. It's supposed to operate as an online scrapbook as opposed to a blog (which my wife Lucy calls it, to wind me up). It's a place for me to put up work in progress, things of interest... whatever really. It's quite a personal project, but everything that goes up there will inform my work in some way.

Project
Futura book
Client
Booth Clibborn
Editions/Mwa
Designer
Ben Drury
Date
2000

I'm guessing that most of your clients are in London or big cities around the world. Yet you live in the countryside, in rural England. How does this affect your work both in terms of your personal creativity and how you deal with clients? It's not much of a big deal. I'm only two and a bit hours away from London, enough distance for me to be in control of my time, but close enough to be in the middle of things at short notice. That distance has definitely benefited my creativity and focus. Now when I go to London, I have a singularity of purpose that I wasn't getting when I was living there. I was too easily distracted and fed up with the grind. Clients don't care where you're working from as long as you make sure you're clear about when you'll be available to them.

What's next for Ben Drury? One of the things I became really aware of when I left London is that if you're not out and about, going out all the time and bumping into people, you slowly become invisible, so I've finally bitten the bullet and am currently developing my web site. I have a signature shoe coming out for Nike, and I'm about to start work on a number of other interesting new projects, some small, some big.

**Project**
Dizzee Rascal—
Tongue n Cheek logo
**Client**
Dirtee Stank Recordings
**Designer**
Ben Drury
**Photography**
Tim and Barry
**Date**
2009

UNKLE
WHERE DID THE NIGHT FALL

NOWHERE
FOLLOW ME DOWN
NATURAL SELECTION
JOY FACTORY
THE ANSWER
ON A WIRE
FALLING STARS
HEAVY DRUG
CAGED BIRD
ABLIVION
THE RUNAWAY
EVER REST
THE HEALING
ANOTHER NIGHT OUT

**Project**
UNKLE promo insert
**Client**
Surrender All
Recordings/UNKLE
**Designer**
Ben Drury
**Photography**
Warren Du Preez
Nick Thornton Jones
**Date**
2007

**Project**
UNKLE—Where Did The
Night Fall lettering
**Client**
Surrender All
Recordings/UNKLE
**Designer**
Ben Drury
**Date**
2010

# How to be a graphic designer, without losing your soul

## Sara De Bondt on graphic design and gender

Sara De Bondt is a Belgian graphic designer who has lived and worked in London since 2002. She studied graphic design at Sint-Lukas, Brussels, Belgium, at Universidad de Bellas Artes, Granada, Spain, and at Jan van Eyck Academie, Maastricht, Holland. She worked first for Foundation 33 and later formed her own studio, which she runs with her assistant Chris Svensson. In addition, De Bondt teaches at the Royal College of Art in London. She co-curated "The Form of the Book" conference at St. Bride Library in January 2009. Her clients include Barbican Art Gallery, The British Council, ICA, Victoria and Albert Museum, Wiels Contemporary Art Centre, Jewish Museum Munich, Nottingham Contemporary, and others. De Bondt's no-frills work is evidence of a clear and precise thinker; her work is at all times characterized by a deep engagement with her subject matter.

saradebondt.com

26 — 28.05.2007

Open
Ouvert
Open

Project
Opening campaign
program brochure
Client
Wiels Contemporary
Art Centre
Designer
Sara De Bondt Studio
Wiels Bold typeface
designed with
Jo De Baerdemaeker
Date
2007

# WIELS

Project
Logo
Client
Wiels Contemporary
Art Centre
Designer
Sara De Bondt Studio
Wiels Bold typeface
designed with
Jo De Baerdemaeker
Date
2007

Project
Luc Tuymans
exhibition signage
Client
Wiels Contemporary
Art Centre (2009)
Designer
Sara De Bondt Studio
Wiels Bold typeface
designed with
Jo De Baerdemaeker
Date
2009

AS:     What first attracted you to graphic design?

SDB:     I wasn't aware of graphic design at all until I had to make a career choice at the end of high school in 1995. My parents pressured me to pursue a university degree in medicine or law, but I was interested in fine art and theater costume design. I visited loads of schools and courses to try to find a solution. At the degree show of Sint-Lukas in Brussels I stumbled into the graphic design department, hidden away at the back of the building. On display were wine labels, record sleeves, and menus, and I remember wondering why you would have to go to school for that. I bumped into the father of a friend, Jef Winnepenninckx, who turned out to be a tutor there. He discouraged me from taking the course, saying I was "too shy."

A few weeks later I took part in their entrance exam anyway. I still wasn't sure what to do but had nothing to lose. I found out I was accepted that same day and enrolled immediately, without informing my parents. Graphic design seemed a good compromise between fine art and university.

Coming from a strict Catholic school where I had been unhappy, I felt at home straight away in the more relaxed and open environment of Sint-Lukas and was excited by the big, messy city surrounding it. The doubts of my family and first tutor Jef were a good catalyst to make me want to prove myself. When I return home nowadays and find myself poring over my parents' collections of cigar boxes, labels, and straw hats, I recognize where my love for design comes from, even if then I didn't realize at the time when I started studying it. I used to spend hours in my tree house when I was younger, making plasticine brooches or marzipan turds for members of my extended family. I think that's why graphic design ended up being a good choice in the end: I like making things for other people.

You studied in your native Belgium as well as in Spain and Holland. How did you end up working in London? In my final year at Sint-Lukas I went on an exchange program to Granada. Despite the fact that it was only for three months and not very productive, the change of scene enabled me to see my degree from a distance and question it. I felt I hadn't learnt enough typography and design history and went on to do a two-year residency at the Jan van Eyck Academie in Maastricht, which was at the time known as a place of reflection on graphic design, with inspiring visiting lecturers and tutors.

In December 2001, during my final months at the Academie, I started to worry about the future and discussed my options with Stuart Bailey, a close friend at the time who had just started a magazine called *Dot Dot Dot* with Peter Bilak. In one of the first issues of the magazine there was a piece by Foundation 33. Stuart urged me to get in touch with them, as some of our work was similar and he knew they were looking for someone. I sent them an email with some jpegs, to which Daniel Eatock replied positively. There was some emailing back and forth with him and Sam Solhaug, and after a visit to London for an interview they hired me.

I moved to London with a suitcase in February 2002, thinking that I would try it out for a year or so before returning to Belgium for a 'real' job. I learned enormous amounts from Dan, Sam, and Hanna Werning and loved working for them, but I felt the itch to be more independent and have direct contact with clients. By a lucky coincidence I got to know James Goggin around that time. He was looking for a studio-sharer and occasional collaborator, a set up that enabled me to quit Foundation 33 and become self-employed.

## How to be a graphic designer, without losing your soul

Do you think designers have to move to one of the world's capital cities in order to be successful? It depends what you mean by successful. To me what matters most is making work you are happy with. Feeling encouraged to grow, to ask questions, and to experiment by clients and peers who share similar interests helps. It adds structure to your practice and gives you a sense of where you want to take it. I think you can find this almost anywhere.

A lot of designers I admire live outside London, in cities like Stockholm, Lausanne, Berlin, Los Angeles, Brussels, Ghent, Madrid, Amsterdam, Seoul, Wittersham, Zurich. The risk of working in a capital city like London is that you begin to believe yourself at the center of the world, to lose that excitement of being on the periphery and feeling that you are not there yet, that you still have to learn.

It's interesting that you worked with Foundation 33, and later with James Goggin. You are often linked stylistically and conceptually with this small group of English designers who work in an unshowy and somewhat pure style, avoiding graphic effects and visual puns. Are you conscious of being part of that group, or is it just an accident of time and geography? I've been told this before, but I really don't feel part of a group, and definitely not an English one. Yes, a lot of my friends are graphic designers, but I wouldn't say that our work is that similar. I feel just as close to designers from other eras or countries.

I meet lots of female students when I visit design schools, but it is less usual to find them in positions of influence in professional life. In the UK, there are lots of female clients commissioning design. You might think this would lead to more female designers, but it doesn't seem to. In the United States, the situation is different; the profession is full of highly qualified, influential women. As a female designer running your own studio, you are unusual. Have you ever found your gender to be a barrier in your career? Being a woman does not automatically grant me a privileged perspective from which to answer these questions. I find it particularly difficult to answer them because I feel that by asking me—as a female designer—about my gender instead of my work, your questions reinforce the stereotype of women as outsiders and men as a neutral, objective norm.

As in most fields, overt gender imbalance in graphic design has undoubtedly diminished. Think of Beatrice Warde, who had to use a male pseudonym to write her articles, "partly because there was one Warde already, and partly because nobody at that time had any idea that a woman could possibly know anything about printing, typography or suchlike."[1] Or Charles Eames, who in 1970 opened his Charles Eliot Norton Lectures at Harvard University with the line: "Ray, who is my wife and not my brother…."[2]

But as you indicate, there are still a lot of stereotypes to unsaddle. At Jan van Eyck a tutor once called my work "too girly," a comment that affected me a lot. When Grafik magazine ran a profile about my studio, a colleague responded by "Ah yes, I heard they were looking for a woman" and when I relayed this story to a second colleague he told me to "stop talking about that again." I still frequently end up as the only female designer on the bill in design conferences[3] and on juries.[4]

[1] John Dreyfus, "Beatrice Warde," 1970 Penrose Annual, p. 71.

[2] "Goods," a talk by Charles Eames during his tenure as Charles Eliot Norton Professor of Poetry at Harvard.

[3] barbican.org.uk/artgallery

[4] awards.dandad.org

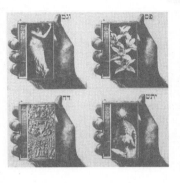

Project
**File Notes (L & R)**
Client
**Camden Arts Centre**
Designer
**Sara De Bondt Studio with
James Goggin (Practise)**
Date
**2004 ongoing**

Project
**Recycled wooden bench
made following Enzo Mari's
Autoprogettazione, part of
exhibition design of Radical
Nature, Barbican**
Client
**Barbican Art Gallery**
Designer
**Sara De Bondt Studio**
Date
**2009**

**How to be a graphic designer, without losing your soul**

5  statistics.gov.uk/CCl

A number of reasons have been invoked to explain the unequal representation of (celebrity) male vs. female graphic designers: from technology (lead typecases were too heavy for women to carry); society (the pay gap in Britain has grown over the last few years);5 the nature of the profession (late deadlines and last-minute problem-solving does not accommodate family life); to women's supposed nature (more shy, less competitive, less self-promotional, more "collaborative").

For me, the only valid reason for this persistent inequality is prejudice, both at the level of individuals and governments. A close friend of mine, an architect, who lives in London and recently had a child, has found out that she will earn more by staying at home than by returning to her job. If a government can encourage women to stay at home, while men face no such pressure, how can we even be surprised of a gender imbalance in the workforce?

Project
Exhibition graphics,
Out of the Ordinary:
Spectacular Craft
Client
V&A Museum
Designer
Sara De Bondt Studio
Date
2008

How does teaching influence your work? I met my assistant Chris Svensson when I was teaching at Central Saint Martins, so teaching has had a major impact on my day-to-day activities.

At the moment I teach one day a week at the Royal College of Art in London. Despite the fact that being away from the studio adds a lot of pressure, I enjoy it enormously. At the RCA I recently started a lunchtime reading group, in part to open up another forum for exchange among students and faculty, but also to force myself to set aside some extra time to read.

I suspect that one of the reasons I like teaching so much is that it is the closest I can get to being a student myself, which is what I would most like to be doing. The same logic applies to my own work: I function best when I feel like I'm learning something from the person I'm working for.

Most of your work is in the cultural sector. Do you envisage doing work outside of the cultural realm? Yes, I'd like to. The work Chris and I are doing at the moment is for the contemporary art world, which is why it tends to seem quiet or understated. When you are representing someone else's artwork—for example in an art catalogue—you don't want to over-power it with your own graphic voice. I would really like to work for fashion or theater, music, or a political party, where the designer can afford to commission or create imagery himself.

You are involved in curating lots of interesting exhibitions and books; *The Master Builder: Talking with Ken Briggs*, for example. How does curating fit alongside your commercial design work? Do you bring a different sensibility to your curatorial work, or is it the same mentality that you employ in your design work?

Though I loved curating "The Free Library" with Mark Owens in London in 2005, *The Master Builder* is a publishing project. Antony Hudek and I started Occasional Papers as a way to spread the word about overlooked moments in the histories of graphic design, art and architecture. The Ken Briggs interview—which I did with Fraser Muggeridge—was Occasional Papers' first book. Our second one, coming out soon, is *The Form of the Book*, a collection of lectures on book design from our conference at St. Bride Library last year. Like teaching, writing, and designing, publishing is a way for me to try to learn, to challenge myself to do and think differently.

With thanks to Antony Hudek.

**How to be a graphic designer, without losing your soul**

Stephen Doyle on graphic design and hiring and employing designers

Stephen Doyle founded Doyle Partners in New York in 1985, with William Drenttel and Tom Kluepfel. He previously worked for Tibor Kalman, and something of the great Hungarian-born designer's spirit can be seen in Doyle's cultured and often witty graphic design. Doyle Partners work in the retail, music, editorial, arts, and corporate sectors. Humor is a recurring theme in the studio's work. In this candid interview, Doyle reveals the enlightened ethos that enables him to find and cultivate designers. He also demonstrates a shrewd recognition of the fact that when he hires good people, they will inevitably leave to start their own ventures. Like all good employers, he is not threatened by this.

doylepartners.com

Project
Look Into the Eyeball
Client
Virgin
Creative Director
Stephen Doyle
Painter
Stephen Doyle
Designers
John Clifford
Ariel Apte
Date
2001

Project
David Byrne at the Apollo
Client
Luaka Bop
Creative Director
Stephen Doyle
Painter
Stephen Doyle
Designers
John Clifford
Jia Hwang
Date
2001

AS:    You worked for the great Tibor Kalman at M&Co, as did Stefan Sagmeister, Alexander Isley, Scott Stowell, and Emily Oberman. That is quite a list—Kalman must have known how to spot talent and how to nurture it. What did you learn from him about employing creative people?

SD:    I learned a lot from Tibor about hiring creative people because on my very first day he fired everyone on his staff but the bookkeeper and told me it was my job to staff the place. Naturally, I hired my friends and my students, notably Alex Isley, who fits into both categories. It is a perfect way to hire, to collect people with whom you want to spend your time. M&Co was a small studio, as is Doyle Partners, and I would venture to say that personality and smarts are more durable than "talent"—whatever that is. Talent is a word that I loathe, because it abdicates responsibility. Having "talent" is comparable to having red hair. It is something perccived as an inheritance, not something one accomplishes. Being a good designer, for me, means that someone is fully engaged in the world, high culture and pop culture, the psychology of the moment, and then brings this framework of understanding as a context for creative work. Often "having talent" can be a masquerade for "having style," which is not as interesting as having curiosity. I try to staff our studio with people who have curiosity and passion. And you must keep a constant lookout for who you might want to hire next, because often the curiosity of our team leads them on to other things. You can't keep brilliance; you let it shine, and then you have to let it go.

As for keeping creative people happy, it doesn't seem so terribly hard, since creative people are generally happy in the first place. At least the ones I hang with are. Creative people need a little room, and everybody needs the chance to fail now and then. Good music and a lot of laughter keep a studio like mine humming along. It's important to have staff who actually like each other, and who are generous with what they care about.

You've had your own design firm since 1985; can you remember what you liked least about being an employee? It's not that I hated not being the boss—what I hated was getting fired. I was fired from my first two jobs, and not for incompetence or unprofessionalism. In fact, it seemed like just the opposite; my bosses were threatened by what I brought to the table, which colored how they were seen by their bosses. My first jobs were in magazines, so the art directors always had to answer to the editors. After my second run-in with the pink slip, a former boss chided me: "You have to make sure you never put yourself in that position again." With that, I realized that it was my responsibility to free myself from any authority who had sway over my creative life. I took one last job at M&Co as a practice run, to see how design studios operated, convinced the whole time that soon I would be on my own.

How many designers are there at Doyle Partners? Doyle Partners has employed close to a hundred designers, but usually just about ten at a time. When we started out, twenty-three years ago, my then-partner Bill Drenttel, who had been an account guy at an ad agency, referred to the designers as "creatives." I quickly broke him of that habit. "If we're the 'creatives,'" I asked, "what does that make you?" I didn't want to have a partner, even a business partner, who didn't think of himself as "creative." Isn't that what this business is all about?

How do you avoid hiring the wrong people? Is there a secret to hiring creative talent? In over twenty years, we have made two wrong hires, and each time I knew, deep down, that it was a mistake. The real secret to hiring designers, if there is one, is to trust your instincts. But that's the secret to the whole profession, isn't it?

I couldn't agree more. So, trusting your instinct, where do you find talent? It rings the bell and comes through the front door. We are in the enviable position that designers seek us out.

**How to be a graphic designer, without losing your soul**

Could you checklist the qualities you look for in a designer? Enthusiasm, appropriateness, curiosity, good footwear, humor, personality, literacy, spell check, manners, and a little sparkle in the eye.

How do you like to be approached by designers who want to get hired by Doyle Partners? Unmarked bills in an interoffice envelope. No, seriously, I can't answer that question, because all the designers who approach us would do it in a certain way, and that would be boring. Plus, the more gullible designers out there would actually believe that there is a "right way" to do something important, like market yourself, and there isn't. And even if there were, it would be different next year. Designers who want to be hired by anyone should do what designers do: consider one's current position, consider one's goals, reflect, and create a way to get from A to B.

Someone once told me to always hire people who ultimately want to start their own studios. I suppose this goes back to your point about knowing that good people will leave and move on. Absolutely. Why would anyone hire someone who wants to be an "employee"?

What is your attitude to individual credits and public recognition of staff? Design is a collaborative effort, or else they would call it art. We credit our work with the name of the company when it goes in front of the public, and that is a survival strategy for the studio. However, within the design world we are happy to credit designers as well as clients who are part of the process of creating work. So why does the studio have my name on it, is that a vanity thing? When we started, I had just left M&Co, which was very hard to spell over the phone. It was the year that the Macintosh computer was launched, and there was no Internet. If people had heard of me, and wanted to hire us to work, they had to look in a phone book, and there we were.

What about non-design staff—do you have admin people? The only admin staffer we have is a bookkeeper. And with a position as important as that, the same rules still hold, except one might also look for signs of organization and fastidiousness. After all, you need to be able to have lunch with your bookkeeper as well as your designers every day, and any personality in a studio of ten to twelve really counts.

How do you reward effort and success? We don't have titles here, and we don't really have roles. I believe that responsibility is never given, but rather taken. In our studio anyone can do as much as they want; the youngest designer can take control of a project and handle a client, if they are up to it. If there is a ceiling at all in our studio, it is simply me.

We share our profits with our staff, to an extent that we think appropriate, and in healthy years the rewards can be positively generous. We offer a fair amount of flexibility for our staff, their hours, whether they work at the studio or at a summer home, and we allow people summers off, say, if they are in pursuit of a dream. But honestly it is neither the finance nor the flexibility that keeps people in this little studio: I think it is being part of a genial group of creative people who enjoy collaborating with each other on behalf of clients that we like, and whose products or services are worthwhile. People stay here because they never know what they're going to get to work on next. Regardless of what it is, somewhere along the way it will capture a sense of adventure and end, someday, with a sense of accomplishment.

Cause an effect.

Project
**Vote poster**
Client
**AIGA**
Creative Director
**Stephen Doyle**
Painter
**Stephen Doyle**
Date
**2001**

Project
**Digital Dollar, for a story about the digitization of money**
Client
**Wired magazine**
Creative Director at Wired
**Scott Dadich**
Senior Designer at Wired
**Christy Sheppard**
Sculptor
**Stephen Doyle**
Date
**2009**

**How to be a graphic designer, without losing your soul**

Paul Sahre on graphic design and illustration

Paul Sahre calls himself a graphic designer, yet much of his work is pure illustration. It's a quality that puts him firmly in the lineage of the great American designer-illustrators such as Milton Glaser, Paul Rand, and Alex Steinweiss. Sahre is based in New York City, working out of what he proudly calls his "shitty office." He received his BFA and MFA in graphic design from Kent State University, Ohio. Today, he combines professional practice with teaching at the School of Visual Arts. His clients include *The New York Times*, Sundance Channel, Knopf, Little Brown, Simon and Schuster, Luaka Bop, *The New York Times Magazine*, *The Washington Post*, and *Esquire*.

paulsahre.com

Project
Aaaaahhhhhhhh!!!!!!!!
Client
New York Times
Designer
Aviva Michaelov
Date
2009

Project
Demonology book cover
Client
Little Brown
Designer
Paul Sahre
Photographer
Michael Northrup
Date
2000

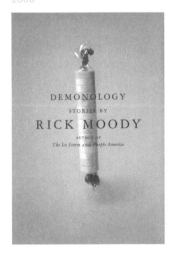

AS:    Can you remember when you first discovered there was something called graphic design?

PS:    I drew a lot as a kid. Super-realistic pencil drawings only: cars, sports figures, pets, flesh-eating demons, stuff like that. I always figured that I would find a way to draw and make a living. While I was in high school my father handed me a book (I don't remember the title) and told me that the book was about "graphic design" and that it looked like something I might study in college. I really had no idea what I was getting myself into until my first few classes at Kent State.

In your early career you had a number of jobs that led to your disillusionment with the role of the designer in modern life. You have described it as being a "cubicle designer." But I wonder if this experience actually made you a better designer in the long run? After I finished school I got married and moved to Baltimore, Maryland. I interviewed at what seemed like every design studio in town and was offered the first of three positions I would hold over a six-year period. At the beginning I was happy to be working and paying off loans, but I became frustrated with the work and the environment. Let's just say that these jobs were nothing like grad school. I was incredibly naive about my expectations. I argued with everyone and basically lied, stole, and cheated to try to do the best work I could do, and I started to wonder about what I had gotten myself into. There were a few bright spots, but mostly it was misery. But yes, in retrospect, I would not trade those experiences for anything, even if the only thing those six years taught me was what to avoid.

You have said: "Graphic design is more than just a job with an in- and out-box and a gray desk. It is about expression and communication." Isn't this what a traditional, service-minded designer—a cubicle designer—would say, too? Yes, and I was by no means suggesting that my experiences, and my likes and dislikes, apply to all designers. Of course they don't. However, I think there are a lot of miserable graphic designers out there, cubicle or not.

In another interview you said: "I personally feel a strong responsibility to comment on what is going on in the world, even though I think in the end graphic designers' attempts have, for the most part, been futile." How do your attempts to comment manifest themselves? It always amazes me that this issue (having an opinion and feeling a responsibility to share it) is polarizing for creative people. Hello, Leni Riefenstahl. To be an applied designer with an opinion obviously means finding clients that have similar opinions or that encourage opinions. Or it's putting opinions into work without the client noticing (rare). Or it's looking for ways to self-author or self-publish. Less obvious, but maybe more important, is the work that a designer says no to.

I look at your work and it seems not to be linked to any tradition or school—do you agree? When I was in college in the 1980s most of the work that I looked up to came from designers with a consistent stylistic approach: April Greiman, *Emigre*, Charles Spencer Anderson, Art Chantry, Rick Valicenti, Michael Vanderbyl, to name a few. But I suppose I remember at one point deciding to actively let the projects take me in different stylistic directions, and I started my career with an "any visual means necessary" mindset.

If it is still happening, then it stems from that, although many people tell me that my work looks like my work, so go figure. I guess what I'm trying to say is that I don't think about it consciously anymore and maybe ideas tie the work together more than execution. There are stylistic patterns to what I'm doing that you might not notice unless you were trying to see patterns. Every once in a while a student will e-mail me asking a question in this regard and I love that someone out there is noticing.

**How to be a graphic designer, without losing your soul**

Can you talk about your non-design influences? 14th Street, my wife, Google, my friends, Village Yogurt, my clients, Dunkin' Donuts, my students, my interns, my office, (the second floor, the fourth floor) my books, my foosball table, and Montauk.

You do graphic design that mixes photography, type, and image, but you also do pure illustration. Not many people do this nowadays, although it used to be common for designers to be illustrators. Is this a deliberate policy on your part? Working the way I do, as a sole practitioner (if you don't count assistants), I survive by diversifying—designing, illustrating, drawing, teaching, lecturing, authoring, printing, publishing, editing, etc. But I have recently had to accept the fact that I don't really have that much control over what work I'm doing at any given time. I can say yes or no to a project, or I can push in certain directions, but in the end, I get work when the phone rings. I think I have always held onto the notion that I have 100% control over the projects I do, but I really think much of it just happens and that's a difficult thing for a control freak like me to accept.

I have been doing illustration (as a graphic designer) since about 1996, when I got my first call from Nicholas Blechman (then at *The New York Times* Op-ed page). One project led to another, but it took years (and literally hundreds of black and white Op-ed pieces) before anyone else called.

In retrospect, I think my "any visual means necessary" approach, which I mentioned earlier, has made it harder for art directors to hire me as an illustrator. But this has changed; art directors who call me are usually comfortable with not knowing how I will execute an idea. So now I do illustration for dozens of different publications—from *Time* to *Golf Digest*.

I did a cover for a book about parallel universes a few years ago, and one of the ideas that stays with me is the "many worlds theory." This states that every decision you make may create a unique alternate parallel reality, with infinite copies of oneself. So there is probably a universe where Nicholas doesn't call me and I end up designing banner ads for a porn site or something.

I'd like to see those banners! But back to illustration: the status of illustration has diminished since its glory days in the 1970s. Nowadays illustration is mainly used as a decorative space-filler. In your opinion, what is the role of illustration today? I know that I have really enjoyed the challenge of "filling a hole" in someone else's layout and not having to worry about anything else. If I was only working that way I would go nuts, but as an illustrator I need to draw and collage and paint and photograph and think conceptually, all with extremely limited budgets and timeframes. Maybe illustration will demand more versatility going forward. The online presence of illustration seems to be more important. Up until now, illustrations I do for print have simply been reproduced online, but the priority has started to switch and online is becoming more important. Maybe this marginalizes illustration even more. Or maybe it gives it another life.

You combine professional life with teaching. How does teaching inform your commercial work? I have been teaching graphic design (part-time) as an adjunct ever since I left grad school in 1990. When we are discussing ideas in the classroom the pressures from the outside world don't apply, leaving my students and me to experiment and push in ways that are difficult or maybe even impossible (at least long term) at the studio. I'm always looking for new ways to allow what I'm doing with the students to affect what is going on in the studio. I would definitely say that the energy and the passion of my students rub off on me, and I hope that this is reciprocal. I teach two classes each semester at the School of Visual Arts (one of these classes meets every Monday morning at my studio), so it is constant and ongoing.

# Interview: Paul Sahre

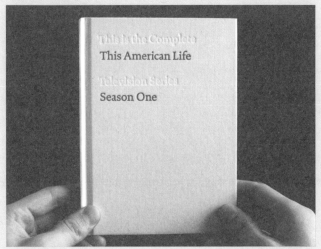

Project
**This Is The Complete This American Life**

Client
**This American Life**

Designer
**Paul Sahre**

Photographer
**Various**

Date
**2000**

Project
**Golf Book Review**

Client
**Golf Digest**

Designer
**Paul Sahre**

Photographer
**Paul Sahre**

Date
**2007**

Project
**Hoop Data Dreams**

Client
**New York Times Magazine**

Designer
**Paul Sahre**

Art Director
**Cathy Gilmore-Barnes**

Date
**2008**

**How to be a graphic designer, without losing your soul**

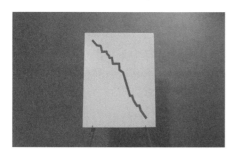

Project
Turning The Economy
Around
Client
Fortune Magazine
Designer / Photographer
Paul Sahre
Sebastian Rether
Date
2007

Project
The Art Of The Tale
Client
Penguin
Designer
Paul Sahre
Sol Hrafnsdottir
Photographer
Michael Northrup
Creative Director
Paul Buckley
Date
2007

Do you have a philosophy of teaching? I don't know if I would call it a philosophy exactly, but I've noticed certain constants in terms of teaching. The one I'm most aware of is my tendency to keep changing as much as I can from semester to semester. I've found that repetition is bad for me. I can't give the same assignment over and over because after a while I start to disengage. This probably makes me a bad teacher, but I work around it by giving assignments that are new to the student—and new to me. This way I stay engaged because I constantly put myself in a position to learn along with the students.

Another constant in my teaching is that I usually avoid hypothetical assignments. If for instance, I assign a logo design project for ABC Bank, I have found that the students end up doing work that seems like it is appropriate for a bank, instead of solving a specific problem. This leads to expected solutions that don't force the students to really confront obstacles.

I agree strongly with this approach. If all projects are hypothetical, it produces students with an odd idea about the role of design in a professional context.

I think most design students can get through four years in a design programme and still not really know the core of the thing that they actually do when they design, which in my view is responding to a series of situations (including deadlines, budgets, content, etc.) and trying to allow each unique situation to produce a unique solution. With no actual client in the classroom as an arbiter, I am by default placed in that role, and I hate being a fake client. I am also bad at it.

Lastly, I have to ask you—on your web site you describe your studio as "shitty"—why? I love my studio. It is located above a Dunkin' Donuts in an old neglected four-story building at 14th Street and 6th Avenue in Manhattan. It's relatively cheap by New York standards, which allows me more latitude in the work I'm doing. It's a dump, but it's my dump.

**How to be a graphic designer, without losing your soul**

Dmitri Siegel on web design

Dmitri Siegel is the web art director for US retail chain Urban Outfitters. He has an MFA in Graphic Design from Yale University. He is on the faculty of the Art Center College of Design in the graduate program in criticism and theory. He also teaches at the University of the Arts in Philadelphia. Alongside his professional design activities, he is creative director of *Ante*, an annual publication devoted to emerging artists and writers, and *Anathema*, a magazine devoted to the pursuit of impossible ideas. He writes extensively on design. His writings have appeared in *Dot Dot Dot*, *Emigre*, *Design Issues*, *Adbusters,* and *The Morning News*.

dmitrisiegel.com

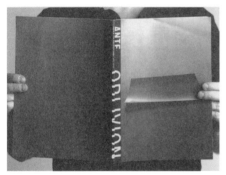

Project
Oblivion (Ante #4)
Client
Ante Projects
Designer
Dmitri Siegel
Art Director
Dmitri Siegel
Photographer
Mathew Monteith (top)
Tom Van Eynde (bottom)
Date
2001

Project
Anathema Magazine
Client
Anathema Magazine
Designer
Dmitri Siegel
Art Director
Dmitri Siegel
Photographer
Noah Shelley
Date
2006

AS:   Can you tell me about your role at Urban Outfitters?

DS:   My title is Executive Director of Marketing. I oversee all the marketing of the brand in North America. We don't do traditional advertising, so marketing at Urban really has to do with making content that is reflective of the spirit of the brand. That content includes the web site, the catalogue, the blog, music programming, and so on.

What would you say is the main difference between an in-house designer and one who works in an independent studio with a variety of clients? Being an independent is like being single—you don't have to fully commit to the relationship with a client. You're playing the field, which shields you from the politics and B.S. of any one client. If there's an awful client you know that you'll be on your way shortly, and it makes it easier to grin and bear it. You can even fire a client!

Conversely, because working in-house is such a commitment, you really need to have a connection to, and faith in, the brand you are working for. You can't just go for some superficial connection or marry for money, because that won't sustain you through the tough times. Not to mention that you will be miserable at your job because you are going to live and breathe that one brand for (hopefully) years. I did not explicitly set out to work in-house, I have just been fortunate to get opportunities with brands like Urban Outfitters and Sundance Channel that I felt really connected to.

As a practical matter, I think in-house jobs are a bit more conducive to a balanced life. That is, they generally pay a decent wage (on a regular schedule) with decent benefits and humane hours.

You make it sound very attractive, and it's true that many independent designers envy the way an in-house designer can work with a single client and develop a position of trust and understanding over a period of time. Is this the best aspect of working in-house? I know what you mean. When I have worked independently you have to play the get-to-know-you games with each new client, whereas in-house that's all done and you tend to focus more on the work. We still struggle with process and trust issues in-house. But as an independent designer some projects can dead-end or go way off track for reasons that you are completely blind to, and that's really frustrating.

For me, the best part of working in-house is that I can influence not just the look of the brand, but the content and the strategy as well. I like having a structural impact, not just a superficial one. Urban has given me the opportunity to go beyond art directing the web site, which was my first job here, and really help shape our overall marketing strategy. Other graphic designers might not be interested in that, but I really think of design as a handmaiden to industry. I'm fascinated by its role in the wider economy.

You mention web design—what makes good web design? Accessibility. It's amazing how immature this medium is. When we do user testing it's clear that people still have an immense amount of anxiety about navigating the web. It's not part of our internal compass yet, like for example the physical store experience that has been refined and perfected over time. We're working on our second decade of the web and as much as there is the temptation to experiment I think that accessibility in terms of technology and design is still the most important element. That doesn't mean that it has to be boring. For example, we did the Urban blog on a horizontal scroll. (I still get angry letters from undergrad graphic designers about this.) It's fine to take that kind of a risk, but then every other element has to be adjusted to accommodate for that. I find this has influenced how I look at print work as well. When I see a horizontal-format book sticking out five inches on the bookshop shelf, it seems vulgar to me now.

## How to be a graphic designer, without losing your soul

What do you look for in web designers you hire? Typographic sensibility is first and foremost on the list, because it's the hardest thing to teach. Beyond that, I have kind of a Freudian approach to designers: I want ids and super-egos. An id designer is an image-maker, someone who can just crank out ideas and variations and is basically raw energy. This generally involves a lot of typos and lack of planning and not a ton of finesse, so I like to balance that with a super-ego designer who is great with typography and systems, sees the big picture, and can figure out how to gracefully execute an idea across multiple media and applications. If I have one of each of these, then I'm all set.

Should a web designer be able to write code? I have come to accept the split between programmer and graphic designer. I fought that for a long time, but I've found exactly one person who was both a great developer and graphic designer. Frankly, particularly on the development side, you don't want a generalist. You want kick-ass, top-notch nerds who love code, and if you compromise that to get someone with a better aesthetic, you pay the price further down the road. Obviously, this approach reflects the fact that I have the budget and the work to employ separate coders and designers.

It seems to me that there is more work for web designers than print designers, and that it would be hard to be a graphic designer today without having a firm grasp of the principles of web design. Is web design the future for graphic design? You wouldn't think so based on the students coming out of design schools! Every recent grad I see just wants to design art books. I think it's a real disservice that design education is giving right now. Not just because those kinds of jobs are so scarce and poorly paying—I could care less about that—but because the web is this exploding and ever-expanding medium and much of that design void is being filled by non-designers right now. The most accessible and widely circulated version of any piece of graphic design is the web site or the jpeg. Design schools need to do a better job of dominating online design, creating excitement around it, and establishing a critical perspective on it.

Does the impermanence and mutability of the Internet mean that web sites can never rival the great pieces of print design that define the graphic design canon? I think this is true. There are plenty of aspects of our culture that are moving to the web with questionable results. I think news has gotten worse as it has moved online, and television is worse on a computer screen. But the transition is inevitable. After ten years of the Internet, I don't think there are many monumental pieces of graphic design online. I don't think it's even clear what the unit of measure is. The field is changing so fast I don't think that we'll be talking about "web sites" in five years at all.

It's funny you mention impermanence though, because I think the web is actually more permanent than print in a lot of ways. You put something on the web and it lives on in a universally accessible form forever. Web design just lacks the institutions like libraries whose sole purpose is to archive and "protect" a canon. (Incidentally, part of the "protection" means making artifacts inaccessible to most people, which is a bit strange.) I wish Google would focus on creating an archive of old web sites rather than scanning books. An archived web site is immune to fire and flood and is also universally accessible.

Interview: Dmitri Siegel

Project
**Russian Art in Translation**
Client
**Ante Projects/DAP**
Art Director
**Dmitri Siegel**
Designers
**Dmitri Siegel**
**Peter Tressler**
Artwork
**Ivan Brazhkin**
Illustrator
**Drew Morrison** (top only)
Type Design
**Tagir Safayev**
Date
**2007**

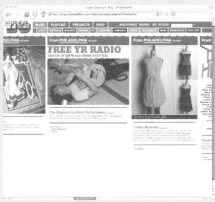

Project
**Urban Outfitters Blog**
Client
**Urban Outfitters**
Art Director
**Dmitri Siegel**
Designers
**Dmitri Siegel**
**Peter Tressler**
**Andy Beach**
**Dan Keenan**
Web
**Ivan Brazhkin**
Date
**2007**

## How to be a graphic designer, without losing your soul

How is usability thinking affecting the design and build of web sites? For me, it permeates the entire design process. The first step of building a web site is the preparation of requirement documents. That's when you think about yourself and what you (or the client) want, and obviously you want people to be able to use the thing. The design process begins in earnest with wireframes and screen-flows. This is the lion's share of the design process and it is incredibly creative. The important thing here is that the graphic designer works on the screen-flows, not just a developer or information architect. In many other offices, the designer gets handed a site that is basically engineered rather than designed and these end up being very soulless. You need to have constant interchange and collaboration between designers and developers. They have so much to teach each other. This process naturally flows into the visual design process. If you have strong wireframes, it's very liberating for the graphic designers; they know that all the user interaction is covered and they can take more risks with the presentation and interaction aspects.

Project
Torched by Mystics Poster
Client
Ditch Projects Gallery/
Ken Miller curator
Art Director
Dmitri Siegel
Designers
Dmitri Siegel
Peter Tressler
Art
Tracy Nakayama
Shana Moulton
Mike Pare
Timothy Marvel Hull
Date
2009

You write about design—how does writing inform your design work? More often my writing is influenced by an experience or insight I have at work. For example, at Urban we decided to stop making canvas tote bags and that led me to write a piece called "Paper, Plastic, or Canvas?" on the broader subject of shopping bags; or I was working on the film titles for a documentary about Dr. Bronner, which led to an article in *Dot Dot Dot* about the label on Dr. Bronner's Soap.

The main thing that writing does for my design work is that it keeps design interesting for me. I think that is one of the biggest challenges for graphic designers—staying interested. Writing forces me to be critical about what I am doing. It forces me to look outside the day-to-day grind of what I am personally doing and reflect on design's place in the wider economy. I think this helps me to continue to take risks and approach design with the same passion that I did when I was a student.

You are creative director of *Ante*, which publishes work by emerging artists and writers, and *Anathema*, a magazine devoted to the pursuit of impossible ideas. Can you talk about these projects? Both of these are print projects that are kind of free spaces for me. One thing I love about design is that you get to learn about all manner of things, because you are designing the book about those things. My Mom was an editor for *National Geographic Magazine* before she retired, so every month she became an absolute expert on the topics she was working on for that issue; I was really inspired by that. *Ante* and *Anathema* give me the opportunity to immerse myself in contemporary art and photography and learn a ton. Again, this is part of keeping it interesting. From a design perspective, *Ante* in particular has allowed me to experiment a great deal and push some ideas on my own schedule.

Both projects are also collaborations with dear friends. Ken Miller is the editor of *Anathema* and Nick Herman is a brilliant artist and my partner in Ante Projects. I am really inspired by both of those guys and learn a lot from them. My social life has always involved working on projects—being in bands, making zines. *Ante* and *Anathema* are the adult extension of that.

You also teach—how does this impact on your professional work? I teach for all the reasons that most people mention: it's a great way to find talent and stay in touch with the next generation, and the energy that I had as a student. But there is something else. I think that teaching is the absolute best preparation there is for managing people. When I first got out of college, I taught drawing and painting at an inner-city public school in New York City. In that situation you have no carrots and very few sticks. You have to motivate thirty people who would rather not be there to do something that they quite rightly perceive to be completely impractical; you have about one week to earn their respect and trust or you are on your ass for an entire year. Compared to that, managing a hundred people at work is a piece of cake! First of all, most of your employees presumably want to be there, and you got to choose who they were in most cases. You can offer them more money and advancement if they do well. In hiring I really value teaching experience because I know that a teacher has been tested in ways that no manager ever will be. People who are good design teachers have a leg up on being great art directors.

# How to be a graphic designer, without losing your soul

## Sophie Thomas on graphic design and sustainability

Sophie Thomas is a London-based communications designer and green activist. She is a founder of thomas.matthews, a consultancy with a growing track record in sustainability in design. The studio's web site notes that: "Our work is always ethically considered and wherever possible, designed for re-use. We specify sustainable materials and processes wherever we can, and seek to source materials locally." She is a co-founder of the campaigning group Three Trees Don't Make a Forest. The group's aim is to "be the catalyst for the creation of a zero carbon design industry."

thomasmatthews.com

Project
Campaign launch of
"No Shop Day"
Client
Friends of the Earth
Designer
thomas.matthews
Date
1998

AS: When did you first know you wanted to be a graphic designer?

ST: I didn't. It found me. I finished my foundation and knew I wanted to go to St. Martin's School of Art, which at that time was a madcap place to study. It was a place where designers who didn't really fit under the traditional heading of graphic design went for three years to experiment. At that point graphic design courses were beginning to change their name to communication design.

Saying that, from the age of around eight I was quite active. I did a lot of posters for CND marches. I was influenced by the graphic work of John Heartfield. CND used graphic design well. They kicked off a lot of political design again following Thatcher.

You worked for the Body Shop: is a period of working in-house beneficial for designers who want to set up their own businesses? Absolutely. I would expect all the work placements who come to me to get a broad range of experience, even if it is for two weeks at a time! Working in a large organization gives you confidence without exposing you to the risks. You have people around you to learn from and, if and when you set up your own business, you have a bit more understanding as to the structure of how to do it—you will have seen a contract for employment or you understand the concept of the job bag. These things are not taught at college.

I'm not sure I would advocate the business model we followed. We had a great working relationship and won a large design contract so we both decided to give up our jobs and set up a studio, which initially began in my living room. So far, so good. But two designers setting up a design business is not an ideal. What you really need is someone with business experience in that mix, thinking about new work, looking for opportunities, keeping the business flowing while the designers do the amazing work. So much of running a business is paperwork, which isn't really what we trained to do.

Tell me the thomas.matthews story.

thomas.matthews started in the canteen at the Royal College of Art. Kristine Matthews and I were sipping coffee from polystyrene cups lamenting the chasm between good design practice taught in the schools and these disposable implements. Kristine's family were based in Eugene, Washington, where everything recyclable is collected and deposited with refunds given for the recovered material. My childhood was often spent marching with my political activist family, so we were well placed to make some "misbehavioral change."

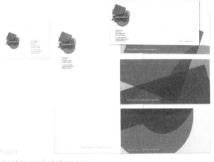

Project
Identity and stationery
Client
Useful Simple Trust
Designer
thomas.matthews
Date
2009

We spent a week going through the canteen records, totting up the amounts spent on polystyrene and disposable items. The figures were shocking. Over 300,000 cups were purchased in a year. Our response was to work with the canteen ground staff to collect a week of waste (5,400 cups and 1,600 aluminum cans). We washed them and hung them in the gallery as a graphic installation. It was very effective. To go with this we designed a mug, which we sold for £2 and negotiated 3p off every time they were used (the cost of a polystyrene cup). The profit we made bought college-wide recycling bins for cans, glass, and paper. We then talked to the waste management company that had the contract to take the RCA's waste and instigated a recycling system that included cardboard. This separation alone saved the college £50 a week.

## How to be a graphic designer, without losing your soul

That was thirteen years ago. After this we showed it around and things snow-balled until we thought we'd better open a bank account.

You now have a well-documented commitment to sustainable design. How does this work in practice? Are you only ever approached by clients with a pre-existing commitment to sustainability, or do you get clients who've never considered the need to act sustainably and just want a smart bit of graphic communication? Many of our clients come to us without knowing our agenda and that is fine. thomas.matthews is not only about sustainability. We encourage everyone in the studio to practise good design and this includes ethically good as well as clever good.

We don't always need to be shouting about sustainability either. Sometimes it is embedded in the practice: a piece of print on a good post-consumer recycled paper; an efficient imposition that allows minimum wastage. These are all design decisions and often not requested by the client.

Clients who are looking for a designer to create an ad for the next 4x4 don't necessarily come knocking at our door, though.

Would you decline an assignment if your client was unprepared to act sustainably? Probably, though not without a fight. I would really want to know what was driving their decision and would probably end up questioning their business model as being very short-term, saying they weren't future-proof.

Here's a slightly different question: if a client expressed a willingness to work within agreed sustainability guidelines and then reneged on the commitment, would you resign the business? Again I would really question the drivers behind such a U-turn. We spend a lot of time with our clients and we build strong working relationships. One would hope that it would become apparent before the change of heart happened that perhaps the client was not as sincere as first thought. There are always alternatives to explore before resignation becomes the only option.

Project
"Me cans" from the
Museum of Me. The
audience were
invited to collect things
in the cans which
were then sealed and
archived
Client
The Sirat Trust
Designer
thomas.matthews
Date
1998–2000

Already some public- and private-sector projects require designers to demonstrate green credentials. Do you see this growing? Yes I do. The notion that regulation restricts creativity is, in my eyes, an excuse, not an argument. Too much choice can have the opposite effect from opportunity and can kill inspiration and creativity. Closing some of those doors could create lateral movements and harder thinking.

The question is what kind of credential, because it needs to be relevant. For instance, why do we still allow redundancy in design? Think about the lifespan of a toothbrush that has been designed for function and looks good in form, but uses four different types of plastic bonded together. It has a useful life of about two months (depending on how avid you are on dental hygiene!), but because of its design cannot be recycled and therefore ends up in landfill with about 400 years of life left in its material composition. That should definitely be wrong.

# Interview: Sophie Thomas

Project
**The Monthly Carbon
Ration Book that
calculates your one
tonne CO2 emission
lifestyle**
Client
**Ministry of Trying To Do
Something About It**
Designer
**thomas.matthews**
Date
**2009**

Project
**Get on Board campaign
that took a bus from
Johannesburg collecting
messages to hand over
to the G8 leaders at
Gleneagles**
Client
**ActionAid**
Designer
**thomas.matthews**
Date
**2005**

## How to be a graphic designer, without losing your soul

What do you say to designers who want to act sustainably yet throw in the towel as soon as a client becomes difficult or uncooperative? As a service industry that needs its clients, we are very good at passing responsibility. But get wise to the demands of your future clients. There is absolutely no doubt that this agenda will return (not that we have seen it disappear) and when it does you will need to be ready. The thing that stops you is lack of knowledge, and knowledge is power. You have to understand the issues and the potential solutions. This allows you to have flexibility when discussing design with clients. A lot of more established designers are wary of this new subject "sustainable design," but in reality a lot of it is good design practice and good communication skills. In graphic design, that would manifest itself in an understanding of print production and imposition and a very good relationship with your printers.

It's often said that clients are way ahead of designers when it comes to sustainability. How do you think the design profession is coping with the need for sustainable action? I believe this to be true. Design is lagging behind on many fronts where we should be leading.

We need to create:
– A new design culture–a new "village" of inspiration, talent, apprenticeship, rivalry.
– A new client culture–creating the next wave of new design success.
– A new consumer culture–an educated, engaged, and enthusiastic home market.

When approximately 80% of the environmental impact is predetermined at the concept and design stage there is clearly action to take. As Kate Krebbs, executive director of the National Recycling Coalition (NRC) in the USA says, "Waste is a design flaw." We seem to be quite good at giving the good glow of greenwash though, which of course must be avoided at all times.

What are the three or four key things a designer should prioritize to function responsibly? Education, education, education. Take in as much as you can. Read things you would not necessarily read and understand the power of your influence. The designer can create demand for a product or service so could also influence your client to do things better.

Understand your process and scrutinize things. Look backwards and forwards. Backwards at the chain of custody of your materials, ask your supplier to hand over information, look for accreditation and standards of best practice. Look forward to the time when your service or product has finished the life it has been designed for and think about where it will end up, then see if you can change the design to make it end up somewhere better.

Once you have done this, tell the story. Many good decisions about sustainability are not apparent. Let people know about your process and be honest about things you could not achieve. Annotation will bring alive sustainability and hopefully inspire people.

Bring on the peer pressure! (You thought it had disappeared when you left school.) Behavior change to the tune of the 80% cut in carbon we have signed up to in the UK by 2050 will no doubt be painful. So, where do we start? We need to get rid of bad practice, to create a shift in the design landscape that makes it unacceptable to do design that is not good.

What are you aiming to achieve with your Three Trees Don't Make a Forest web site?

All of the above. I am always astounded that communication designers say they have no impact. They are, after all, only designing one A6 [4 by 6] postcard. They don't connect with the 200,000 that are being run off the press. With over 550,000 tonnes of direct mail going into the waste stream every year in the UK, that is some serious impact.

Three Trees talks a lot about the designer's sphere of influence. You may think you design in isolation when you sit in front of your computer, but think of your community, your clients, your suppliers, and then think of who they connect with and then their connections. We are not islands; we are vital nodes in a complex connected system, a system that now needs to shift up into the eco-efficient gear.

Page 1
British Council
Pavilion for Glastonbury,
a collaboration with
Structure Workshop
engineers
Client
British Council
Designer
thomas.matthews
Date
2005

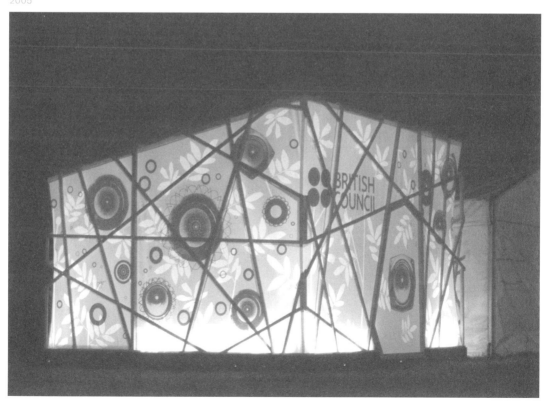

**How to be a graphic designer, without losing your soul**

Magnus Voll Mathiassen on graphic design and starting a studio

Magnus Voll Mathiassen was a co-founder of the uber-hip Norwegian graphic design studio Grandpeople. The studio became widely celebrated for their highly distinctive, illustration-based style of graphic expression. The company worked for leading youth brands and record labels, and were extensively written about in the international design press. In 2009, Voll Mathiassen quit Grandpeople and set up MVM, a new solo venture. He is based in Drammen in Norway, and continues to work for a wide range of international clients.

themvm.com

Project
Stian Westerhus
"Galore" – Gatefold LP
with fanzine
Client
The Last Record Company
Design
Magnus Voll Mathiassen
Date
2009

AS:    When did your interest in design start?

MVM:    With the ZZ Top record *Afterburner*. I was six years old and it gave me an instant urge to draw. I didn't know what graphic design was until I started at the Bergen National Academy of the Arts and Design, when I was aged twenty-one.

How did you come to form Grandpeople? We were three guys who met at the Bergen Academy. We discovered the possibilities of graphic design and all the limitations and control set by the profession itself. We were young, and this gave us the typical DIY spirit and energy that formed us as a group. We got a moniker to work under and continued the collaboration after graduation.

What was the biggest obstacle you encountered in getting Grandpeople started? Money. We didn't have any start-up loan to float on and we didn't have enough well-paid jobs. It was hard, but we had the mentality to go with it. Some might say the stupidity to do it.

Was getting Grandpeople off the ground more or less difficult than you imagined? I have nothing to compare it with. It gradually got better and better. The first two years were the hardest, and I told myself that if this doesn't work out financially by the third year, then I'm out. But it started getting better. On a creative level it was always good, and we learned a lot, especially in the first years.

You got some good press coverage early on; did this open doors? We were flabbergasted when *Grafik* magazine wanted to do a ten-page profile on us just months after opening the studio. It still makes me wonder how that happened. We thought this was our ticket to international clients and some money. But it definitely wasn't. I think potential clients want to see a progression in a studio's portfolio before deciding to work with them. The people who got in touch were students, and after a while different magazines and publishing houses wanted us to contribute to various publications. It took more than one or two years before we got contacted by real clients as a result of the publicity. Fame is mostly talk. You need to convince people over time that you can do real and strong work.

What were the main issues relating to being part of an equal partnership? Would it have been easier if it had been just you and a couple of assistants, or were there advantages in being a group? Being close friends and starting up together has been the recipe for both success and failure. We knew everything about each other's preferences and so easily worked out a conceptual and aesthetic foundation for Grandpeople. The disadvantage was that we found it difficult to be frank with each other when we had disagreements. With friends working together, starting young and becoming older, you grow apart on many levels. In the long run it would have been easier to work in another constellation.

What were the main objectives behind Grandpeople? Creative freedom? Financial reward? Respect from other designers? Creative freedom, and a refusal to work behind regular office walls or in an established design studio. We wanted to see if our ideas would fit into the world of graphic design and our surroundings.

At a key point, you moved out of the Grandpeople studio and into your own studio, but continued to work as part of Grandpeople. Why did you do this? There are many reasons. One of them was that the city the studio was located in was too rainy for me. Rain all year around. But the main reason is internal issues of running the studio and the history we have had together. I needed to get away to be able to work with my colleagues and friends. And this became the beginning of the end of my part in Grandpeople.

**How to be a graphic designer, without losing your soul**

Project
Soft Metal Model –
T-shirt print
Client
Grandpeople
Design
Magnus Voll Mathiassen
Date
2009

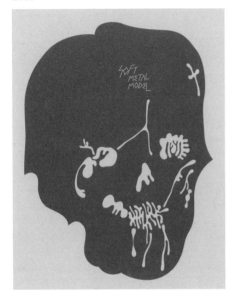

Project
Vagant cover and
illustrations
Client
Vagant Magazine
Designer
Magnus Voll Mathiassen
Date
2009

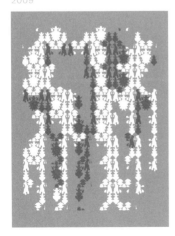

**You have now made a clean break and are working solo under a new studio name—MVM. Can you talk about your thinking?** It's a fresh start—my own work, my own hours, total control over every aspect of running a business. I am a person with strong opinions—which is both a good and a bad thing. And now knowing that I can execute things in a specific way gives me a feeling of freedom again. Saying that, I need to feel that what I do is a direct consequence of my own actions. I am a focused person, and working on my own, I need to always be on the tip of my toes, which is essential to attract the clients I will click with. It's the feeling of being an eternal student that keeps this profession interesting. No one knows anything, even if you have your opinions and your gold awards or such things. MVM will be my university with no possibility to graduate.

**It doesn't sound as if you will ever employ other designers. Is that the case?** Over time, MVM may evolve into being a studio with employees. I am open to that, but for now I will only use freelance artists or collaborate with people, as well as doing projects solo. I like working with people and exploring all the creative forces around. Digital communication makes this very easy, even if you are situated in an unknown small city of Norway, as I am.

**Would you do anything differently if you could start all over again?** With the knowledge I've gained over the past years I would never have adopted the approach we took with Grandpeople. But it has been a very valuable experience, with many ups and a few downs.

Starting with friends is a risky business, and the design business is a risky business itself, so make sure you have total confidence in the people you will be working with. Be honest and don't dwell on any conflicting issues you might have. You will just end up sour as an apple.

**What will you do differently (if anything) with your new venture?** With MVM there is a proper direction from the beginning. I know what is ahead and I know my preferences. If MVM gets recognized as a provider of distinctive work, rather than a distinctive aesthetic, then two thumbs up.

**If you could give someone starting up a new studio one piece of advice, what would that be?** Be patient and eat healthily.

**How to be a graphic designer, without losing your soul**

Jonathan Barnbrook
*Barnbrook Bible:*
*The Graphic Design of Jonathan Barnbrook*
Booth-Clibborn Editions, 2007

Anthon Beeke, Nick Bell, Ken Cato
and others
*Area*
Phaidon Press Ltd, 2005

John Berger
*Ways of Seeing*
Penguin Classics, 2008

Michael Bierut
*79 Short Essays on Design*
Princeton Architectural Press, 2007

Hugues Boekraad
*My Work is Not My Work:*
*Pierre Bernard—Design for the Public Domain*
Lars Müller Publishers, 2008

Ben Bos, Elly Bos
*AGI: Graphic Design since 1950*
Thames & Hudson, 2007

David Brittain
*Eduardo Paolozzi—The Jet Age Compendium:*
*Paolozzi at Ambit 1967–1980*
Four Corners Books, 2009

Wim Crouwel
*80 20 100*
Nijhof & Lee, 2008

David Crow
*Visible Signs:*
*An Introduction to Semiotics*
AVA Publishing, 2007

Daniel Eatock
*Imprint*
Princeton Architectural Press, 2008

Stephen J. Eskilson
*Graphic Design:*
*A New History*
Laurence King, 2007

Robin Kinross (editor)
*Anthony Froshaug:*
*Typography & Texts, Documents of a Life*
Hyphen Press, 2008

Karl Gerstner
*Designing Programmes*
Lars Müller Publishers, 2007

Kenya Hara
*Designing Design*
Lars Müller Publishers, 2007

Steven Heller, Lita Talarico
*Design Entrepreneur:*
*Turning Graphic Design Into Goods That Sell*
Rockport Publishers, 2008

Steven Heller
*Design Disasters:*
*Great Designers, Fabulous Failures,*
*and Lessons Learned*
Allworth Press, 2008

Mark Holt, Hamish Muir
*8vo—On the Outside*
Lars Müller Publishers, 2005

Richard Hollis
*Swiss Graphic Design: The Origins and*
*Growth of an International Style 1920–1965*
Laurence King, 2006

Richard Hollis
*Graphic Design: A Concise History*
Thames & Hudson, 2001

Andres Janser, Barbara Junod
*Corporate Diversity:*
*Swiss Graphic Design and Advertising*
*by Geigy, 1940–1970*
Lars Müller Publishers, 2009

Christoph Keller, Stuart Bailey, Ryan Gander
*Appendix Appendix*
JRP|Ringier/Christoph Keller Editions, 2007

Robin Kinross
*Unjustified Texts:*
*Perspectives on Typography*
Hyphen Press, 2008

Alan Livingston, Isabella Livingston
*The Thames & Hudson Dictionary of Graphic*
*Design and Designers*
Thames & Hudson, 2003

Ruedi Baur, Irma Boom, Julia Hasting and others
*Area_2:*
Phaidon Press Ltd, 2008

Ellen Lupton
*Thinking with Type:*
*A Critical Guide for Designers, Writers,*
*Editors, and Students*
Princeton Architectural Press, 2004

John Maeda
*The Laws of Simplicity*
The MIT Press, 2006

Karel Martens, Paul Elliman, Carel Kuitenbrouwer
*Counterprint*
Hyphen Press, 2008

Roger. L. Martin
*The Design of Business:*
*Why Design Thinking is the Next*
*Competitive Advantage*
Harvard Business School Press, 2009

Philip B. Meggs, Alston W. Purvis
*Meggs' History of Graphic Design*
John Wiley & Sons, 2006

Bill Moggridge
*Designing Interactions*
The MIT Press, 2007

Bruno Munari
*Design as Art*
Penguin Classics, 2008

Lars Müller, Victor Malsy
*Helvetica Forever:*
*Story of a Typeface*
Lars Müller Publishers, 2007

Donald A. Norman
*Emotional Design:*
*Why We Love (or Hate) Everyday Things*
Basic Books, 2005

Rick Poynor
*No More Rules:*
*Graphic Design and Postmodernism*
Laurence King, 2003

Rick Poynor
*Obey the Giant:*
*Life in the Image World*
Birkhauser Verlag AG, 2007

Rick Poynor
*Jan Van Toorn:*
*Critical Practice*
010, 2008

Norman Potter
*What Is a Designer:*
*Things, Places, Messages*
Hyphen Press, 2008

Lucienne Roberts
*Good Ethics of Graphic Design*
AVA Publishing, 2006

Emil Ruder
*Typography:*
*A Textbook of Design*
Niggli Verlag, 2009

Stefan Sagmeister
*Things I Have Learned in My Life So Far*
Harry N Abrams, 2008

**How to be a graphic designer, without losing your soul**

Paula Scher
*Make It Bigger*
Princeton Architectural Press, 2005

Adrian Shaughnessy
*Graphic Design:*
*A User's Manual*
Laurence King, 2009

Adrian Shaughnessy
*Cover Art By:*
*New Music Graphics*
Laurence King, 2008

Adrian Shaughnessy
*Display Copy Only:*
*A Book of Intro Work*
Laurence King, 2001

Adrian Shaughnessy, Tony Brook
*Studio Culture:*
*The Secret Life of the Graphic Design Studio*
Unit Editions, 2009

Edo Smitshuijzen
*Signage Design Manual*
Lars Müller Publishers, 2007

*Peter Saville:*
*Estate 1–127*
JRP|Ringier, 2007

Gemma Solana, Antonio Boneu
*Uncredited:*
*Graphic Design and Opening Titles*
Index Book, 2007

Deyan Sudjic
*The Language of Things*
Allen Lane, 2008

John Thackara
*In the Bubble:*
*Designing in a Complex World*
The MIT Press, 2006

Alice Twemlow
*What is Graphic Design For?*
RotoVision, 2006

Rudy VanderLans
*Emigre No. 70 the Look Back Issue:*
*Selections from Emigre Magazine 1–69.*
*Celebrating 25 Years of Graphic Design*
Gingko Press, 2009

Judith Williamson
*Decoding Advertisements:*
*Ideology and Meaning in Advertising*
Marion Boyars Publishers, 1978

Laetitia Wolff
*Massin*
Phaidon Press Ltd, 2007

*Beauty And the Book:*
*60 Years of the Most Beautiful Swiss Books*
Arthur Niggli, 2004

*Wonder Years:*
*Werkplaats Typografie 1998–2008*
ROMA Publications, 2008

# How to be a graphic designer, without losing your soul

**How to be a graphic designer, without losing your soul**

This book is dedicated to Katy Richardson, my former business partner. As each year passes, I realize more and more how lucky I was to have her as a partner during my fifteen years of Intro.

Thanks to my new business partners Tony Brook and Trish Finegan who put up with me being a semi-detached member of the Unit Editions team during the writing of this new edition.

Heartfelt thanks to my interviewees: Jonathan Barnbrook, Sara De Bondt, Stephen Doyle, Ben Drury, Paul Sahre, Dmitri Siegel, Sophie Thomas, and Magnus Voll Mathiassen.

Thanks as always to Laurence King, Jo Lightfoot, and Felicity Awdry for patience and encouragement and the hard work they put into making the first edition of this book such a success. Thanks also to my editor Sophie Page for gracefully putting up with my missed deadlines and late copy.

Thanks to Jonathon Jeffrey, Mason Wells, Tim Beard, and Tom Munckton at Bibliothèque for the updated design. As always, working with Bibliothèque was rewarding and—well, good fun.

Special thanks to Stefan Sagmeister, who remains the patron saint of this book.